Church lighting

Peter Jay and Bill Crawforth

Church House Publishing
Church House
Great Smith Street
London
SW1P 3NZ

ISBN 07151 7584 X

Published 2001 for the Council for the Care of Churches of the Church of England by Church House Publishing.

Copyright © The Archbishops' Council 2001

Cover design by Visible Edge

Typeset in Sabon 10pt

Printed in England by
Halstan & Co. Ltd
Amersham, Bucks

All rights reserved. No part of this publication may be reproduced or stored or transmitted by any means or in any form, electronic or mechanical, including photocopying, recording, or any information storage and retrieval system without written permission which should be sought from the Copyright and Contracts Administrator, The Archbishops' Council, Church of England, Church House, Great Smith Street, London SW1P 3NZ. (Tel: 020 7898 1557; Fax: 020 7898 1449; Email: copyright@c-of-e.org.uk).

Contents

Illustrations and Tables	iv
Acknowledgements and Note on the text	v
chapter 1 Introduction	1
chapter 2 Fundamental considerations	4
chapter 3 Project planning	13
chapter 4 Light sources	20
chapter 5 Lighting fittings (luminaires)	33
chapter 6 Design	40
chapter 7 Controls	55
chapter 8 Maintenance	63
chapter 9 Conservation and safety	67
appendix 1 The measurement of light – photometry	70
appendix 2 Glare	77
appendix 3 Colour	79
appendix 4 Contract clauses	82
appendix 5 Precautions with dimming systems	84
appendix 6 Bibliography	87
Background information	88
Index	89

Illustrations and tables

All photographs and diagrams except numbers 5, 13 and 14 were taken or drawn by Bill Crawforth, who is the copyright holder.

fig. 1	Crisp shadows given by sunlight enable details of the church to be seen clearly.	5
fig. 2a – f	Lighting of a preacher's face from various angles	6–7
fig. 3a & b	An east window where stained glass has been replaced by clear glass, so unbalancing the distribution of interior light.	10–11
fig. 4	A typical drawing of a detailed lighting layout.	18
fig. 5	Electrified candelabra at Ely Cathedral. Photographs © McCloud & Co. Ltd.	38
fig. 6	Badly chosen and sited downlighters.	41
fig. 7	Inappropriate lighting obscuring the details of altar furniture and casting unwanted shadows.	44
fig. 8	Lighting of the choristers' faces and music.	44
fig. 9	Lighting the choir from standards.	45
fig. 10a & b	Lighting a reredos.	46
fig. 11a & b	Lighting a reredos.	47
fig. 12	Measurement of the direction of a beam of light.	50
fig. 13	A good example of external floodlighting. Photograph © NEP Lighting Consultancy	52
fig. 14	Floodlighting which fails to bring out the form of the buttresses and other features. Photograph © Mark Wood-Robinson	52
fig. 15	The concept of solid angle.	71
fig. 16	Diffuse, spread and specular reflection.	75

table	
Comparison of possible light sources.	32

The Authors

Bill Crawforth OBE MSc BA MSLL originally trained and worked as an architect and then studied lighting at the Bartlett School of Architecture.

Peter Jay MA FCIBSE FSLL CEng FConsE originally trained as a scientist, and formed Peter Jay and Partners, consulting engineers dealing with all building services, but specializing in lighting and controls.

Acknowledgements

The authors wish to express their thanks to the following who have made many valuable suggestions and comments:

Professor James Bell, Richard Gardner, David Loe, J. A. Lynes, Derek Phillips and Professor Joseph Rykwert.

Note on the text

Bold or bold italic type has been used in this guide to highlight 'essential information'.

chapter 1
Introduction

The aim of this guide is to help parishes decide whether the lighting in their church can be improved, and if so, in what way. It also discusses how to seek advice and commission a design, and describes the requirement for various approvals before starting work. Although it has been written primarily for the clergy, members of Parochial Church Councils (PCCs) and other interested non-specialists, it may also be of value to technical specialists in clarifying the particular needs of churches. It is not a textbook, and avoids technicalities where possible, although certain basic matters are explained in appendices.

The accounts of the Origin of the Universe given by Genesis and the 'Big Bang' theory in physics both accord light a position of primary importance. Further, light has always been a symbol for what is good, or should be striven after, as opposed to darkness symbolizing what is bad or to be avoided. Light is therefore particularly important in buildings intended for religious worship, but this does not necessarily mean the indiscriminate use of high-intensity illumination.

In early churches, structural and economic factors restricted the size of window openings. Up to the thirteenth century, glass was very expensive and window openings in country churches were often left unglazed or covered by oiled parchment or other translucent material. Such openings were therefore kept to the minimum size in order to limit draughts but, in any case, maximizing the *quantity* of light was not considered of primary importance. Where daylight was insufficient, votive candles and sanctuary lamps, usually of oil, fulfilled the needs of both religious symbolism and visibility.

Stained glass came to be used in the early Middle Ages, long before large windows were possible. It was primarily intended to embellish the interior by 'painting with light'. From the twelfth century onwards the flying buttress and other structural inventions of church builders made it technically possible to provide larger and larger windows. However, this did not generally lead to greater amounts of daylight, but often to the increasingly elaborate use of stained glass which can tell a story or emphasize particular features and always provides unending variety and interest as the daylight falling on the exterior varies: the constant flickering and movement of candle flames supported and added to the sense of movement in the lighting.

In the great medieval churches of Europe the combination of arrays of beeswax candles with stained glass windows, often emphasized by the glitter of mosaics, plus painted sculpture and woodwork, attained a variety and sophistication in the creative use of light never surpassed in the western world.

In Mediterranean countries the generally brighter skies and longer hours of sunshine ensured that church interiors, even with the same restrictions of size and glazing material, were much lighter than in north-west Europe, and the attitude to daylight depends very much on climate. In particular, direct sunshine is generally excluded from buildings in hot countries.

The destruction of stained glass windows after the Reformation, increasing with the rise of the Puritans and accelerated during the English Civil War 4of the seventeenth century, led to an increase in daylight in churches where windows were replaced with clear glass and not, as sometimes happened, simply filled in. English churches from the seventeenth century onwards required relatively high levels of daylight in order that personal contact between preacher and congregation could be maintained and so *quantity of light* became a significant factor in church architecture. The need for lighting to enable the congregation to read their service books in comfort inside a church did not arise until the nineteenth century. Before then most people were illiterate, and those who were not probably knew much of the Bible and services by heart. Standards of interior illumination were very low by present-day standards, even in the houses of the well-off, and people were accustomed to making an effort when reading indoors.

More than this, it was not considered necessary for the congregation to be able to follow all the details of a service and for this reason good daylight in the sanctuary was rarely regarded as important, especially if providing substantial windows with clear glass might interfere with other aspects of design. In some churches in the UK the tradition was continued well into the nineteenth century, reinforced by the Oxford Movement with its emphasis on traditional 'Catholic' ritual.

As soon as town gas became a practicable means of interior illumination in the early nineteenth century it began to be installed in urban churches. At first gas lighting used batwing burners, as the Welsbach gas mantle was not invented until 1885, and resembled a more controllable kind of candle – the sources were yellow and flickered in a draught like candle flames, but could easily be increased or decreased by opening and closing a simple tap. Both candles and gas lamps created considerable heat, soot and smell, although the church demanded beeswax candles in place of tallow until, in the nineteenth century, both materials were largely replaced by paraffin wax.

When, in its turn, gas came to be replaced by electricity the whole character of the light changed. Electric lamps do not move and are of constant intensity unless special measures are taken to dim them. When first introduced in 1878 their advantages were mainly in convenience in turning on and off, and in freedom from dirt, smell and risk of fire. The light itself was not regarded as an improvement, and electric lighting was (and is) often described as 'hard' compared with flame sources. The invention of the gas mantle made gas appear superior to the early 'light bulbs' in many respects, and at the time considerably cheaper. However, as electric lamps gradually improved, it became possible to obtain much more light than is practicable with candles or gas, without at the same time producing excessive dirt and discomfort.

The relatively gradual replacement of gas by electric lighting in the last decade of the nineteenth century coincided with a great increase in literacy and the decline of rote learning so that more and more people could read,

but fewer and fewer were able to follow a church service from memory. For the first time it became necessary to have enough light in churches for the whole congregation to read easily. New styles in architecture also involved many changes in new building.

Other mainly liturgical changes followed, such as the movement to make the sanctuary clearly visible from the nave, or to move the altar westward, while baptismal pools are now being installed in an increasing number of churches. In buildings of traditional form there are often considerable difficulties in attempting to add lighting appropriate to these relatively new requirements without conflicting with, or intruding on, the architecture.

During the last 60 years there has been a bewildering increase in the number and type of electric sources available. Most of the newer discharge sources are represented as being more 'economical' than the older filament lamps, but often have disadvantages such as a difficult shape, a strange colour, or availability only in large and rather awkward wattages.

Although there have been many successful church lighting installations of recent years there have also been many disappointments, often where bright 'floodlighting' has been installed at the expense of proper emphasis and subtlety. Parishes may be unsure where to seek advice and become confused between conflicting promises of brighter light, reduced costs and ease of maintenance.

Most churches have an inspecting architect/surveyor but although the architect's advice will be invaluable, only a minority would claim much detailed knowledge of lighting technique. A few electrical contractors have a special interest in lighting, but most would expect to take the advice of equipment manufacturers and suppliers who too often tend to believe, quite sincerely if mistakenly, that their newest product is inevitably the best. Further, the majority of lighting specialists, whether employed by manufacturers, suppliers or consultants, deal mainly with shops and other types of commercial enterprise and may be genuinely unaware of the very different needs of churches.

Virtually all churches will need specialist advice, independent of any particular manufacturer or other purely commercial interest. Various people describe themselves as 'lighting consultants' or something of the kind but this term is not protected, and many might more accurately be called manufacturers or salesmen. The Chartered Institution of Building Services Engineers (CIBSE) publishes a list of lighting consultants who are independent of commercial connections and have achieved a required standard of qualification and experience. However, not even all of these are experienced in ecclesiastical work, and it is by no means suggested that enquiries should be confined to this list. Choice of a professional adviser should ideally result from a combination of recommendation and interview: the Diocesan Advisory Committee (DAC) may be able to advise, as may other parishes with a successful installation.

The appointment of specialist advisers is also discussed in Chapter 3.

chapter 2
Fundamental considerations

The purposes of lighting in churches

The most obvious purpose of lighting in any building is to enable the occupants to see clearly what they wish and need to see, but there are fundamental differences between churches and most other kinds of building. First, the fabric of the church and many of its elements have a symbolic function. This may sometimes be expressed in exceptional height, structural daring, cruciform plan and so forth, but even small and simple churches and chapels convey a message: the lighting should never detract from this message but, at its best, assist it.

This is sometimes referred to as 'revealing the architectural form' or some similar phrase, but it goes far beyond this. The requirement is not merely to reveal particular architectural details but to show how they contribute to the total impression of a building intended for religious worship. In addition, light itself is a symbol, as explained in Chapter 1, and in appropriate cases this symbolism should be developed.

Second, the focus of interest in a church constantly varies. During the course of an ordinary service attention may move from the building as a whole to the centre aisle, then to the chancel, the choir, the pulpit, the lectern, the books of the congregation and then back to the choir and perhaps to the sanctuary. For special services the focus may be a side chapel, the font or a procession in the aisle. Apart from this, of course, the clergy and congregation should always be able to see each others' faces and expressions clearly.

One solution to these varied requirements might be to ensure that all parts of the church are brightly lit at all times when the building is occupied, and there are some churches where this has been done. However, in any but the smallest, uniformly bright electric lighting is likely to be intrusive, since few traditional churches were designed with this kind of lighting, whether by day or by night, in mind. Moreover, it is obviously desirable that the lighting should assist people to concentrate on whatever is most important at any particular part of the service, and simply drenching the building with light, which might be quite effective in a shop or office, may create a totally unsuitable atmosphere and involve unnecessary expense.

To some extent the requirement for differing emphasis on different parts of the building at different times can be dealt with by suitable arrangements of switching or simple dimming controls. Nevertheless, continual alteration of the lighting during a service may well be distracting, and few parishes are likely to have the skill and personnel to do anything of this kind really well.

Great care is necessary in placing and directing the light to make sure that the building, people and objects inside it are seen clearly and naturally, and without distraction from overbright light sources, whether these be windows, candles or electric lighting.

Another purpose of lighting in and around a church, too often neglected, is that of security. Where intruder alarms might be thought inappropriate (or, in rural areas, ineffective) lighting which comes on automatically as people approach or enter a church and which can be seen from a distance can often act as a deterrent from crime. Further, the roads and paths leading to churches should wherever possible be lit at night when in use by the congregation and visitors.

Many churches are floodlit, and when the floodlighting is in use it is likely to provide enough light both for security and access. However, floodlighting is normally turned off at 11 p.m., or possibly at midnight, and there may be a need for separate security lighting at other times.

Floodlighting can be valuable in drawing attention to a church, especially if it is of architectural merit, and so increasing interest in a building which might otherwise be taken for granted. In particular, church towers and spires used to dominate towns, but are now often dwarfed or obscured by higher buildings. Floodlighting can do much to redress the balance.

fig. 1
Crisp shadows given by sunlight enable details of the church to be seen clearly.

Photograph © Bill Crawforth

Emphasis and modelling

Particular features of a church can be emphasized in many different ways, but overall bright lighting cannot contribute to the effect.

Emphasis of particular objects by creating contrasts in shape, colour or texture with their surroundings is a commonplace of design, and lighting can help by ensuring that they are seen accurately. Brighter lighting can help as well, but bright lighting of something which is itself quite uninteresting or insignificant often does more harm than good. The extreme example is to point a narrow beam spotlight at a plain white wall: the patch of light invariably looks as if some mistake has been made, as in fact it has.

fig. 2
Lighting of a preacher's face from various angles.

Photographs © Bill Crawforth

(*a*) from behind

(*b*) from below

(*c*) from the side

Fundamental considerations

(d) from directly overhead

(e) casting a shadow on the background

(f) with 'natural' light

Modelling by lighting consists in emphasizing the three-dimensional shape of objects by highlight and shadow, which means that the light must reach the object predominantly from a limited range of directions. Where the light is totally diffuse, as in the open air from a fully overcast sky, modelling from the lighting is absent: it is no accident that we generally choose to photograph buildings in bright sunshine which creates crisp shadows (*see figure 1*).

Our concept of 'natural' modelling is based on the fact that daylight is generally somewhat diffuse, and comes from above and from one side: faces, particularly, can look positively unpleasant if lighted from below, especially by a small source which casts sharp shadows. Lighting on faces from vertically overhead can also be disagreeable and should be avoided (*see figure 2d*). Further, the piers, arches, vaults and ribs of Gothic architecture are designed to be seen in daylight, and when they are lit from unusual angles distorting shadows and disruptive patterns can be created.

Totally symmetrical lighting on, for instance, the altar, may make it look flat and dull, and some variation in the lighting from one side to the other is nearly always desirable. The special problems of lighting particular features are discussed in Chapter 6.

Lighting for reading

As explained in Chapter 1, lighting sufficient to enable the congregation to read their books easily is a relatively recent requirement in churches, but difficulty in reading is nowadays one of the commonest complaints, especially from the elderly.

Reading is one of the very few visual tasks in a church which requires lighting on a horizontal, or near horizontal, plane. Nearly everything else the congregation wish to see – the faces of the clergy and choir, the pulpit, the reredos and so forth – are effectively vertical surfaces. It is possible for one system of lighting to perform both functions satisfactorily, but separate sources must often be provided.

Quantity of light – visual performance

As measured by instruments the range of lighting conditions over which we can see adequately is very wide indeed: effectively from dawn through full sunlight, to dusk and even bright moonlight. However, we can see fine detail much better where the lighting is bright than where it is dim. Although we might be able to make out the headlines in a newspaper under bright moonlight, we could hardly read the whole text. Further the amount of light required to see detail of any particular size increases markedly with age.
In the early days of electric lighting, a great deal of research was devoted to finding relationships between the amount of light falling on unit area of a surface (called *illuminance*) and ease of seeing measured in various ways. This was to decide how much 'expensive' electric light was worth paying for in factories and offices.

Although the economics of lighting have changed dramatically, far too many lighting specialists still think of the illuminance on a notional horizontal 'working plane' (usually conceived as a desk or bench) as the most important aspect of a lighting installation. There are recommended figures for the illuminance of various parts of a church (see Appendix 1). However, as noted above, it is only for the books of the congregation that *illuminance* should be measured on the horizontal; in most other cases we are interested in vertical surfaces. Lighting for the music and books of the choir forms a special case which is discussed in Chapter 6.

In general, older people require more light than younger ones for a given ease of seeing, but there are some eye conditions found among the elderly where more light does not help. Where the lighting is good enough for those with satisfactory eyesight and only those with poor vision complain, it may be worth considering providing books or service sheets in large print for the latter. Where there is a copier with facilities for enlarging, or better still, a desktop publishing programme, this can be quite easy to do. For certain problems this may be more effective than providing more light. This is a highly complex matter and for particular cases advice from ophthalmologists or possibly optometrists might be sought.

Electric lighting in relation to daylight

As explained in Chapter 1, in many older churches the provision of large amounts of daylight was not originally thought important, and even where there were large windows they were, and may still be, glazed with stained glass which lets in little light. Further, in some churches daylight in the chancel and sanctuary is deliberately kept at a low level, either by small, or densely coloured stained glass, windows.

There are cases where there was originally a large stained glass window which, owing to damage or for other reasons, has now been replaced by clear glass, thus totally unbalancing the provision of daylight throughout the building (*see figures 3a and 3b*).

The relationship between daylight and electric lighting in churches may therefore vary over a very wide range. In some cases electric lighting is required only when daylight fades, but in others it is needed much of the time when the building is in use to correct an imbalance between the lighting of one area and another.

Daylight always enters from windows and roof lights and flows towards the interior. To this extent it may be said to be coherent and ordered. Electric sources are nearly always inside the building and where they are located near the outer walls there can be an ordered flow of light, as for daylight. However, a series of chandeliers or other sources hanging inside a space do not necessarily create an ordered flow in the same way. This will be discussed in Chapters 5 and 6.

One rather special case is the use of electric lighting to illuminate stained glass from the outside. For instance, a stained glass east window may be the focus of interest during the day, but becomes black at night. This may not matter where the only light inside the church is from candles or sanctuary lamps with perhaps a little light on the altar, but can mar the appearance of

fig. 3
An east window where stained glass has been replaced by clear glass, so unbalancing the distribution of interior light.

Photographs © Bill Crawforth

(*a*) by day

the whole church if this is otherwise well lit by electricity. In such a case it may be desirable to provide floodlights outside the east window to prevent its appearing dark. The possibilities and pitfalls of doing this are discussed in Chapter 6.

Dramatic use of lighting

Words such as 'dramatic' and 'theatrical' are often used of church lighting both as terms of approval and disapproval. In this guide the term 'dramatic' will be used of lighting which is intended to heighten the emotional impact of the building or a service, which most would regard as desirable. The word 'theatrical' does not necessarily imply approval or disapproval, but merely draws an analogy with techniques of lighting used in the theatre: as many lighting designers gained their interest and early experience in the theatre their use of such techniques is hardly surprising, and whether this is a good or a bad thing depends only on the result.

However, where it is thought that the use of theatrical techniques is to vulgarize or trivialize the impact of a church service, the appropriate term

(b) the same, by night

of disapprobation is 'stagey' and this terminology will be followed in the remainder of this guide.

The basis of dramatic lighting is to create substantial contrasts between those elements which it is intended to emphasize and other things which may be less important. As explained above, it is not sufficient merely to light something brightly, for what is lit must be interesting and significant in itself. Further, whereas in the theatre it may be effective to concentrate the light on a very small area (a single actor or dancer, or perhaps even only on a single face), this is out of the question during a church service.

While it may be desirable to concentrate lighting on the sanctuary or around the altar during a service, it is not desirable to confine the light too closely since the officiant has to be seen clearly when moving about. More intensely dramatic lighting may be acceptable when the church is not in use for a service, and concentration of light on some particularly striking feature, such as a rood, may be effective for visitors or for those assembling for a service.

Old and new churches

In this guide most attention will be paid to the problems of lighting older churches, never originally intended to be lighted by electricity, or indeed to have much light after dark at all. Similar principles apply to modern churches of relatively recent date with effective electric lighting already, although it may be desirable in some cases to change to the more efficient equipment that has become available in the last few years.

There is, however, a substantial number of churches that were provided with electric lighting when built, but in which the illumination is quite inadequate by current standards. Where these are of traditional form the principles applicable to historic buildings can be followed, but those of unusual design require specific inventive solutions which may differ from conventional designs, but should still provide adequate glare-free lighting and accord with the other basic principles set out in this guide.

chapter 3
Project planning

The following chapter covers the various stages of a project for lighting a church, whether a new or an existing building. It can also act as a check-list for both professionals and members of a PCC who have had experience of organizing work in their church. Those matters more relevant to existing rather than new buildings are indicated in the text.

Need for new lighting

New lighting in an existing building usually follows the realization by the congregation that the existing lighting fails to meet their needs.

- Insufficient light has been mentioned in Chapter 1, but it is rare for action to be taken for this reason alone.
- Changes in ritual or reordering may have altered the positions towards which the lighting should be directed.
- The need to renew or extensively repair the electrical installation may prompt a decision to replace lighting fittings, which may have deteriorated through age to the point of failure, or for which replacement parts may no longer be available.
- Health and Safety legislation may have rendered the replacement of lamps and general maintenance at high level too expensive when using a contractor or too dangerous for a parishioner.
- A desire to economize on the electricity consumed by old inefficient fittings is frequently expressed, but the cost of replacing the fittings to save electricity can rarely be justified when lighting is used only for a few hours weekly. This is covered in Chapter 4.

The existing installation

If the existing lighting is considered unsatisfactory it is useful to check whether the installation is working as it should.

- Are all the existing fittings actually working, or pointing in the right direction?
- Are they in need of cleaning?
- Measuring the level of light (the *illuminance*) provided by the existing installation can identify those places where more light is needed, and so establish whether new work is really necessary.
- It is not unusual for an existing installation to provide a level of light in the nave less than half that now recommended.
- Many contractors have meters for measuring illuminance (*photometers*), but they can also be hired.

The possibility of fitting lamps of higher wattage into existing fittings may be considered, but technical advice will be needed to ensure the following:

- Both the wiring and the fittings can sustain the higher electrical loads and the extra heat generated.

- A sample should be tested to ensure that the change does not produce glare (see Appendix 2).
- The capacity and quality of the electricity supply to the church should be checked to establish whether it can support an increase in the load from lighting, particularly if discharge lamps are to be used.

With this information a decision can be made whether to adjust the existing lighting, to supplement it, or to replace it. When existing decorative fittings are to be retained for aesthetic or historical reasons, it is important to establish the extent to which their light output can contribute to the final scheme (see Chapter 5).

Brief

For both new buildings and new installations in existing buildings the PCC should always prepare a brief which states what they wish the lighting to achieve. While this guide, and especially Appendix 1, includes recommended standards for the average installation, only the users can clarify the particular needs of their own church. All activities in the church should be listed. They may include:

- services of different kinds taking place in various parts of the building
- choir practices
- meetings
- concerts
- plays
- flower festivals
- cleaning

The style of all normal services, and the character of the environment required should be stated – whether bright, tranquil, subdued, etc.

The brief for an existing building should also say whether or not lighting is required for the daytime, and whether it should then be noticeable. It may be desirable to modify the daylight, for example by screening an over-bright east window, or shading intrusive sunbeams.

The brief should state whether it is required to alter the lighting during a service, and whether this can be done by switching or whether dimming equipment is needed, and should also define the positions from which to operate the switches or other controls. It should state whether different sections of the church are to be lit at different times, whether lighting is to be available whenever the building is open, and if time switches or presence detectors are required. Controls required for exterior lighting, whether floodlighting, footpath, car park, or security lighting, should also be considered (see Chapter 7).

An experienced lighting designer should be aware of such points, but cannot necessarily be expected to know how to apply them in the circumstances of a given church, nor to foresee requirements that are unusual. It is helpful if they have been considered before meeting the lighting designer so that possible options can be discussed. At this stage it should also be decided who will represent the PCC in contacts with other bodies such as the DAC, the planning authority, and eventually the contractor, since failure to do this at an early stage will result in confusion and possibly increased cost.

Consultation

The organizations with which the PCC and their designer must consult are the same for lighting as for any other project in a church.

- The DAC can give advice and direction in the early stages, and must receive the proposal as a preliminary to requesting a faculty from the diocese for the work.
- Although the Church of England has exemption from listed building control, planning law still applies and discussion with the local planning authority about any work outside the building is necessary.
- It is impossible to give general guidance on the previous point, since each planning authority is free to determine its own policy. Some insist on a formal planning application for all changes, but others assume that any work for which a faculty has been granted will be acceptable.
- English Heritage (see Appendix 6) and other historical bodies may be involved, particularly where rare artefacts are concerned, whose preservation is dependent on protection from light or from the process of installation.
- External work, and occasionally internal work, may involve the attention of archaeologists, particularly if trenching through a churchyard or opening up a floor void is involved.
- The church's insurers may have specific concerns.

The requirements of all these bodies may have to be incorporated in a designer's brief or contractor's specification. The inspecting architect/ surveyor and the DAC can advise regarding the bodies to be consulted. In particular, the DAC may refer relevant applications for a faculty to statutory and historical bodies, who may have a representative on that committee, and will encourage early consultation. (Addresses are given in Appendix 6.)

Design

Once the brief has been agreed it must be developed into a design which a contractor can execute. Although Chapter 6 gives general advice about design, it is not a detailed design guide, and in practice somebody with technical knowledge has to prepare a design and arrange to have it carried out. Who is chosen to do this depends on the extent of the work.

Where only the addition of the odd extra light is needed, such as spotlights on the altar, and it is generally agreed where they should be located and how switched, it may be sufficient to ask an electrical contractor who knows the church to submit a quotation. Few such contractors claim much knowledge of lighting, and most are likely to seek the assistance of a lighting manufacturer or distributor, most of whom offer a 'free' design service. However, it must be remembered that 'free' designs, from whatever source, are likely to have been prepared by junior staff, and may often be worth exactly what has been paid for them. Even in the simplest case of this kind it is generally desirable to carry out a trial, and if it is successful the installation can be cleared with the diocese and completed without further ado.

Engagement of a contractor by nomination, rather than by selection after obtaining competitive tenders, is not recommended where more than £300

or £400 worth of work is involved, except in those (in our experience rare) cases where a professional electrical contractor is an active member of the congregation and is known to carry out work virtually at cost as a gesture of goodwill.

It is necessary to be particularly careful with the DIY amateurs who are anxious to 'save the church money' by their own time and effort. However well-meaning, this normally costs a great deal in the long run. Even people with real professional knowledge who are not actually working in contracting may well find it difficult to obtain the right components and are likely to have to pay retail prices for materials, so vitiating much of the notional saving.

Where competitive tenders are sought it is essential that all firms price on the same basis, and there must be a detailed description of what is required. Preparing suitable drawings and a written specification is a specialist matter, and unless there is a suitably qualified member or friend of the congregation with the knowledge to do it properly, and the enthusiasm to do it without charge, it must be done professionally and paid for. The still common practice of asking a 'favoured' electrical contractor to prepare a specification which is then sent out to tender is to be deprecated. It is both unfair and unbusinesslike, since other contractors, knowing who is 'favoured', often do not bother to prepare a proper tender, while the favoured contractor is aware of being exploited and may react accordingly.

As pointed out above, electrical contractors rarely have the skill to prepare a good lighting design, and are likely to be over-influenced by Part L of the Building Regulations which apply to new buildings but not in this context to new, or at all to existing, churches. (See Appendix 6 for the application of the Building Regulations.)

The inspecting architect/surveyor is likely to be among the first to be approached for a lighting design. Not many architects or surveyors have a detailed knowledge of lighting technology, and although an increasing number of practices include staff with a professional knowledge of building services they do not necessarily cover lighting. However, if the architect's or surveyor's own staff cannot provide the expertise, they may well be able to recommend other firms who can.

As explained in Chapter 1, the term 'lighting consultant' is not protected by law, but the CIBSE publishes a list of properly qualified lighting consultants who are independent of commercial connections. However, not all are necessarily experienced in church lighting, and enquiries need not be confined wholly to this list. The choice of a professional adviser ought to be by a combination of recommendation and interview. Apart from the architect, the Council for the Care of Churches, the DAC, and other parishes with successful installations may be able to suggest names for interview.

Specification

As explained above, to obtain the maximum benefit from competitive tendering it is essential to have a complete and clear specification with drawings. These will include plans and schedules detailing what is required and where it is located (*see figure 4*), and a description of the amount, nature and location of the wiring. The booklet *Wiring of Churches* (Andrew Sage, 1997) describes the standard required, and so protects against shoddy workmanship, but it does not identify equipment and controls which must be specific to the particular church.

Additional to the clauses mentioned in *Wiring of Churches*, the extra clauses relating specifically to lighting listed in Appendix 4 should be included in the specification.

Tendering

Three tenders are probably sufficient for work of moderate extent in the average parish church, but for relighting and rewiring a large church or abbey five may be more appropriate.

- Contractors invited to tender should be enrolled with the National Inspection Council for Electrical Installation Contracting (NICEIC).
- DACs may have a list of contractors found satisfactory in other churches, otherwise the experience in church work of all contractors invited to tender should be investigated.
- To ensure that competition is genuine at least one non-local contractor, and not necessarily the same one every time, should be invited to tender.
- In addition to the technical competence of contractors it may sometimes be desirable to investigate their financial standing.

Competitive tenders can show substantial variations in prices, but after checking, and referring back a suspiciously low tender for confirmation (not revision), the lowest tender should be accepted. The value of an installation in a church is usually low by comparison with general commercial work, and the cost of preparing a proper tender is quite significant. It is therefore unreasonable to invite an excessive number of contractors to tender for any given job.

Installation

The following matters should preferably be dealt with in the specification (see Appendix 4), but if not they should be discussed and agreed before a contract is placed:

- access for both contractor and congregation;
- duration with start and completion dates, and the implications for scheduled and other church services;
- clearing away for services and other activities (such as choir practice) in the church;
- temporary lighting and its switching;
- storage for materials and equipment, particularly for lighting and dimming equipment for which the parish may have paid;

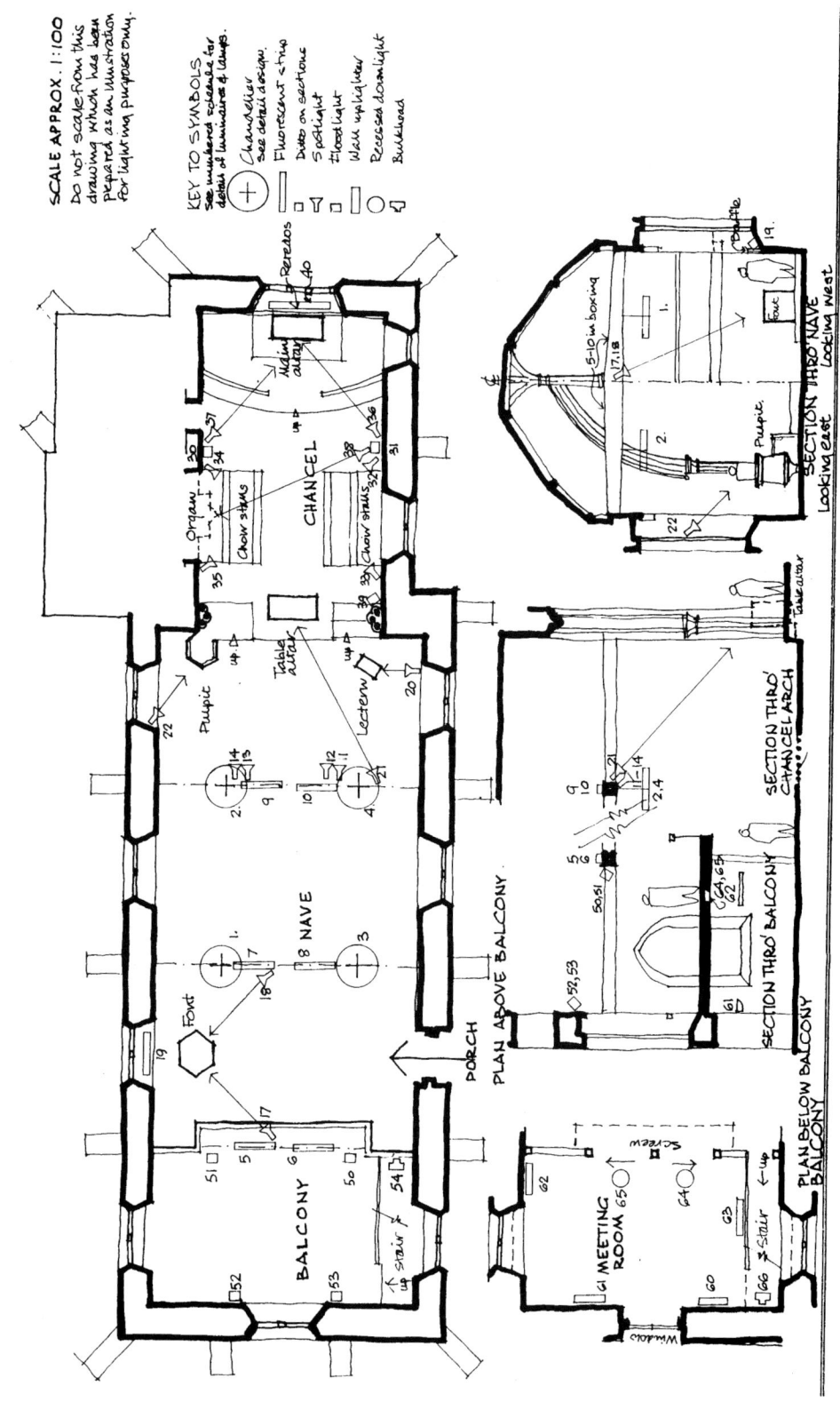

fig. 4
A typical drawing of a detailed lighting layout.

© Bill Crawforth

- protection of the fabric, particularly intrinsically or historically valuable items;
- archaeology and the action to be taken if a 'find' is made;
- cable routes should be confirmed in detail;
- other planned works not forming part of the contract, but which may impinge on it.

The following should be dealt with before work starts:

- The church's insurers should be informed.
- The installation of new lighting in a church is unlikely to be either sufficiently costly or lengthy to justify action under the Construction (Design and Management) (CDM) Regulations, but this should be checked. (See Appendix 6 for further information on these regulations.)
- Appropriate safety measures must in any case be defined and responsibility for their observance agreed.
- Interference with the contractor by members of the parish other than the agreed representative should be discouraged.
- When the inspecting architect/surveyor is involved all parties should agree on a procedure for dealing with queries from, and instructions to, the contractor.

chapter 4
Light sources

AUTHORS' NOTE Light sources are developing rapidly, particularly under pressure for a 'greener' environment. What follows, written in 2000, will rapidly become out of date. To assist those who are not concerned with detail, Table 1, at the end of this chapter, summarizes the information.

There are two different kinds of electric light source: *incandescent* and *discharge*.

- With the incandescent type electricity is used as a source of heat to raise a fine metal wire (the *filament*) to such a temperature that it gives off light.
- Discharge lamps operate on a completely different principle, that of an *electric discharge* through a gas.
- Depending on the nature of the gas, its pressure and various other factors, this discharge may give off visible light directly, or *ultraviolet (UV) radiation*. The latter is not itself visible but can excite certain types of chemicals, called *phosphors* to give off visible light in their turn.
- Where a substance absorbs one type of radiation and gives off another this is called *fluorescence*.
- Many gas discharges emit both visible and UV radiation together.

For incandescent lamps the process is essentially ***electricity → heat → light*** and is governed by rigid physical laws which limit both the *efficacy* (that is, the amount of light emitted for each watt of electricity consumed) and the life of lamps.

- The higher the voltage applied to a filament the more light it emits, but the shorter its life.
- Incandescent lamps always give out far more energy as heat than as light, and means have to be found to dissipate this heat (which also has to be paid for along with the light).

For discharge lamps the processes ***electricity gas discharge → (1) visible light and/or (2) UV radiation → phosphor → visible light*** are more complex, but do permit the manufacturer to manipulate the parameters in many different ways.

- There is therefore a wide range of discharge lamps available, most of which give off far more light (and rather less heat) for a given electricity consumption than incandescent lamps.
- Discharge lamps can also be designed to have very long lives.
- As against this, discharge lamps are essentially complex and therefore expensive to manufacture.
- They require *control gear* to ensure that the discharge starts and is properly maintained.
- Most are difficult to dim.
- For many there is a delay in giving full light output after switching on.
- However, perhaps the most serious limitation of discharge lamps for use in churches is their effect on coloured objects, or ***colour rendering*** (see below for further details).

There are two main problems connected with the use of discharge lighting in churches: the first is prejudice from people who have had unfortunate experiences with unsuitable lamps in the past and are therefore unwilling to consider them at all. The second, and perhaps more common problem nowadays, is an unthinking acceptance of what is 'new', 'modern' and 'economical', particularly in churches where access for maintenance of the lighting is difficult and the very long lives of some discharge sources appear to reduce the problem. As will be discussed in later sections, there are other ways round the problem of maintenance.

Colour of light

White light is a complex mixture of all spectral colours from red to violet which can be separated as in a rainbow or by a prism. Objects which appear white reflect all colours equally. Those which appear coloured reflect some colours more strongly than others.

We perceive the colours of objects in accordance with the proportion of the different spectral colours reaching our eyes from them, but this obviously depends not merely on whether, for instance, the object reflects red more strongly than blue, but also on the composition of the incident light. For instance, an object which appears bright red in ordinary white light might appear dull if the light itself were deficient in red.

The real problems come with those objects whose appearance depends on a subtle balance between different colours, as for flesh tones. Their appearance can vary markedly with the composition of the incident light, and people will often complain that particular sources make colours appear distorted. There is also the phenomenon known as *metamerism*, in which two surfaces which appear to match under one type of light source no longer match under another type. For this reason it is always best to try out light sources with the actual materials and in the real interior in which they are to be used. Trials with colour samples and the like may be misleading.

The balance of colours in daylight can vary markedly. Taking an overcast sky as the standard, sunlight is a good deal yellower, while a clear north sky is bluer. Most flame sources, like candles and oil lamps, are very markedly yellow, while incandescent lamps are intermediate between candles and sunlight. Curiously, although the composition of the light reaching our eyes from coloured objects will vary enormously from under an overcast sky to bright sunlight and so forth, we are rarely disturbed by this, although we are aware of it. Even with candles and incandescent lamps we do not complain that colours are distorted, although they often make blues look rather dull.

It appears that where the spectral composition of the light differs from natural white light in a regular way we can make allowance for this and, in view of the marked variation in colour of daylight from sunrise to sunset, a visual system which could not do this would be of rather limited value. Not merely daylight but also most flame sources vary from white in such a way that we can compensate for them.

However, the spectral composition of many discharge sources does not vary from white in a regular way, but may have peaks and gaps in different parts of the spectrum and the visual system cannot make allowance for these. For this reason we often perceive colours under these lights as distorted. As noted above, this applies particularly to flesh tones and other colours whose appearance depends on a balance between various parts of the spectrum. There is also the risk of metamerism, as described above.

It is important to know how well or badly a light source displays colours and two indices are required for this purpose, neither being sufficient by itself:

- The first is *correlated colour temperature (CCT)* which indicates whether the source is 'warm' (that is, yellowish) or 'cool' (that is, bluish). An incandescent lamp has a CCT of about 2,700° and sunlight about 4,000°. *Paradoxically, the 'higher' the colour temperature the 'colder' the light: the light from the north sky has a CCT of 8,000° or more.*
- The second figure to describe the colour performance of a light source is the colour rendering index (Ra). Colour rendering means the way in which the light source affects the appearance of coloured objects. An index of 100 implies complete accuracy while an index of 60 or less is poor. Sources with an index above 80 should be used for churches.

However, it is important to distinguish between colour rendering and colour appearance – the latter describing how a light source looks when viewed directly. In practice most sources, even those of poor colour rendering, appear something approaching 'white', and it is impossible to judge the colour rendering of a source merely by observing its appearance.

It cannot be emphasized too strongly that colour rendering and colour appearance are highly complex phenomena and trials should be conducted *on site* whenever it is proposed to use an unfamiliar source.

The explanation of colour given here is as brief and simple as possible. A more extensive discussion is given in Appendix 3.

Incandescent lamps

These are variously referred to as incandescent, filament or tungsten lamps – tungsten being the usual material from which the filament is made: it is invariably wound into a tight spiral.

- The pear-shaped 'light bulbs' commonly used in the UK for domestic and local lighting are called General Lighting Service (GLS) lamps and are normally fitted with bayonet caps (BCs).
- In most other countries screw caps (ES) and lampholders are used, as they are for the larger sizes in the UK (Goliath Edison Screw (GES)).

Incandescent lamps are available in a wide range of shapes and sizes for special and decorative purposes.

- Among the most common are various types of 'candle' lamp, some literally shaped like candles, some merely approximating the outline of an idealized candle flame. These are sometimes used in churches for choir

stall lighting, or in chandeliers, wall brackets, etc. but their performance is generally inferior to that of GLS lamps of the same wattage.
- Linear incandescent lamps are available and are often used for picture lighting, in small brackets over reading desks and for lighting in showcases. Their life tends to be limited, and they should be distinguished from linear fluorescent tubes to be discussed in a later section.

An important class of incandescent lamp is those with integral reflectors, which are mushroom shaped.

These come in two types, the simple reflector spot with a thin blown glass envelope and the thicker glass 'pressed glass aluminized reflector' (PAR) type, more generally useful in churches.
- They direct their light not all round but only in one defined direction.
- The reflector is sealed within the lamp and cannot become dirty, as external reflectors invariably do.
- Many of these lamps are available in both 'spot' and 'flood' versions, and it is important to state which is required in any individual case.

For some lamps there is a choice of several different beam spreads, and not just two.

Tungsten-halogen lamps

As stated above, the hotter a tungsten filament the more light it emits but the sooner it breaks. The mechanism of breakage is that the white-hot tungsten literally evaporates from the filament and over time is deposited on the inside of the glass envelope of the lamp, which is a great deal cooler. Where GLS lamps burn with the cap upwards the blackening of the glass is around the neck, which minimizes the loss of light, but where burning with the cap downwards the blackening causes loss of light. As metal slowly evaporates one or more points on the filament reduce in diameter and become hotter, so losing more metal by evaporation. Eventually the filament breaks at one of these 'hot spots'.

Tungsten-halogen lamps have a small quantity of iodine, bromine or occasionally fluorine, in the envelope: these chemical elements, plus chlorine, form a group called the *halogens*, hence the name. All form chemical compounds with the gaseous tungsten which remain a gas at moderate temperatures but at higher temperatures break up into their elements again. Where the parameters are exactly right tungsten is not then deposited on the inside of the glass, which is hot enough to keep the compound gaseous although stable, but back onto the filament, which is hot enough to break the compound up.

Mains voltage tungsten-halogen lamps give about 25% more light than GLS lamps of the same wattage, and can be designed to last two or three times as long. They were originally made for special uses, but their range and use are increasingly being extended.

Most of the PAR and reflector spotlights in common use are now available in tungsten-halogen form, and in most applications it seems likely that they will eventually displace the non-halogen types of reflector spot.

Miniature reflector-type tungsten-halogen lamps

To obtain a closely controlled beam of light it is necessary to have the smallest possible source directed by a lens or reflector or both. Wire filaments operating at low voltage are shorter and can therefore be wound more compactly than mains voltage filaments, which means that lamps operating at 6 or 12 V can be both smaller and the light more closely controlled than mains voltage lamps of equivalent light output. Further, the filament will be thicker and can therefore be run at a higher temperature without shortening its life.

Tungsten-halogen reflector spotlights designed for operation at 6 or 12, and occasionally 24 and 35 V, etc. are now commonly used for display lighting. They are very small and can therefore be fitted into a neat enclosure, while the transformer to provide the low voltage can be mounted remotely. It is sometimes said that a 50 W 12 V tungsten-halogen spotlight gives as much light as a 120 W mains voltage PAR 38 lamp, but this is untrue. It gives at most half the amount of light in total. However, the centre of the beam of the 50 W 12 V lamp is almost as intense as the centre of the 120 W PAR 38 beam and for shop window displays, etc. this may be all that matters.

By contrast with display lighting, in churches where reflector spotlights are used the light from outside the main beams of many sources can be very important. For instance, a common way of lighting the nave is to mount PAR spots in groups at eaves level, behind corbels, etc. The beams of different spotlights will overlap and as a result, only half or less of the light at each seat may come from the spotlight pointing directly at it, and the rest is built up from light outside the main beams of several others. The walls and arcade are also likely to be lit largely by this 'spill' light.

The life of incandescent lamps

The properties of tungsten filaments are governed by rigid physical laws, one of which is that the life of a given filament is greatly shortened if the applied voltage is increased, while the light output goes up; the effects are reversed if voltage is reduced.

- Most GLS lamps are designed for a nominal life of 1,000 hours at their rated voltage.
- 'Long life' lamps with a rated life of 2,000 hours or more are also available.
- The longer the rated life the lower the light output for a given wattage, but this may not always matter very much.
- Mains voltage tungsten-halogen (T-H) lamps are generally designed for rated lives of 2,000 or sometimes 3,000 hours, while low voltage T-H lamps are often rated for 4,000 hours or more.
- PAR 38 lamps are rated for a 2,000-hour life.
- Blown glass reflector spots are rated for a 1,000-hour life, but they are notorious for not always achieving this.
- As noted earlier, non-halogen reflector types may be displaced by tungsten-halogen in the long term.

The 'rated life' of a given type of lamp means the average life of a large batch tested under controlled conditions of voltage and so on. As stated above, lamp life is sensitive to voltage and, in country churches particularly, this may vary a good deal, being low at peak periods such as winter evenings and high at other times when the demand on the rest of the electrical system is low. In practice, the mains voltage in a church which may be in use at times of low demand elsewhere is likely to be high during services, and this may have an adverse effect on lamp life. The problem can be dealt with by using dimmers as discussed in Chapter 7.

Discharge sources

The discharge lamps which are at present (2000) worth considering for interior lighting of churches can be classified into six main groups:

(a)   (hot cathode) linear fluorescent tubes
(b)   shaped and compact fluorescent lamps
(c)   high-pressure sodium lamps
(d)   metal halide lamps
(e)   induction lamps
(f)   light emitting diodes (LEDs)

Types (c) and (d) are often grouped together as *high intensity discharge (HID) lamps*.

Hot cathode linear fluorescent tubes

These are the straight tubes commonly used for office and shop lighting, etc. and are often referred to as 'striplights' and occasionally (incorrectly) as 'neon lamps'. They come in standard fixed lengths from 150 mm (6 in) up to 2,400 mm (8 ft) and may be from 16 mm ($^5/_8$ in) to 38 mm ($1^1/_2$ in) in diameter. The most common in the past have been 1,200 mm (4 ft), 1,500 (5 ft) and 1800 mm (6 ft) long and 38 mm diameter. However, these are being displaced for new installations by tubes of 26 mm (1 in) diameter, and 16 mm diameter in the smaller sizes. All such tubes give more light than incandescent lamps of corresponding wattage and burn for 5,000 hours or more.

Tubes are described by a code giving the diameter of the tube in units of $^1/_8$ in. Thus a 26 mm (1 in) diameter tube is a T8 and a 38 mm ($1^1/_2$ in) tube is a T12.

Hot cathode tubes should be distinguished from 'cold cathode' tubes which are longer, up to 3 m or more, and can be bent to shape. 'Cold cathode' tubes are sometimes used in supermarkets etc. but have negligible application in churches. In the remainder of this guide the term 'fluorescent tube' will be used to mean the hot cathode type only.

Fluorescent tubes are available in a range of colours intended for different applications. Originally there was a conflict between the requirements for good colour rendering and high light output, but during the last few years the so-called 'tri-phosphor' tubes which combine high light output with a colour rendering index (Ra) of 85 or more have come on the market, at a range of correlated colour temperatures from 2700° up to 6,000°. This type should always be used in churches, while it has been suggested that the older types should be withdrawn, or even made illegal.

Owing to their shape these tubes are often difficult to use in the main body of a church, although they have been used to light recesses where there is an arched opening to screen them, or above cornices, while on occasion special screening has been added to window embrasures in order to conceal them. They may also be very suitable for lighting ancillary spaces, such as choir vestries, sacristies, offices, etc.

All fluorescent tubes require control gear, which is normally housed within the fitting or *luminaire* (see Chapter 5).

- Where these tubes are used on their own the control gear can be housed nearby.
- The gear is generally about 200 mm (8 in) long by 50 mm (2 in) square in section.
- It gives off some heat and may hum, so mounting positions must be chosen with care.
- Radio frequency emissions from wiring between the control gear and lamp caps may interfere with public address systems, and this wiring should be screened with metal and kept reasonably short.

Shaped and compact fluorescent lamps

The length of linear fluorescent tubes prevents any but the shortest, with limited light output, being used where relatively small sources are required, as in table lamps, circular recessed ceiling fittings, etc. Development has concentrated on forming the tube into 'compact' shapes which are easier to handle. Tubes formed into a circle have been available for many years and may be more suitable for use in vestries and similar places than the straight tubes. U-shaped tubes have also been available for a long time, but not until recently in small sizes.

There is now a large variety of so-called *'compact fluorescent lamps'* (CFLs) available. These employ glass tubes of small ($^1/_2$ in, 12 mm) diameter formed into multiple hairpin, ziz-zag or spiral shapes of various kinds so that the whole source is comparable in size with an incandescent lamp and can be used as a direct substitute for it. Some have the control gear concealed within the lamp and can be fitted directly into a bayonet or screw lampholder, but in that case the control gear is discarded when the lamp fails. Other types use a special adaptor containing the gear, which can outlast several lamps. In either case, the control gear is electronic in operation and much smaller than that for standard linear tubes.

CFLs typically consume only one-fifth as much electricity as incandescent lamps of equivalent output, and last 5,000 hours or more. Some are rated for 10,000-hour life, but they are relatively expensive to buy. However, their low heat output can be a great advantage in applications such as desk and table lamps. Most are available in two colours, 'warm' and 'cool', and their main disadvantage is that many cannot at present be dimmed, and most take a minute or more to reach full output after being switched on.

CFLs can be a very useful substitute for incandescent lamps in applications where the lamp cannot be seen directly. For use where the lamp can be seen types are available with a complete frosted envelope which can usually fit

into a space intended for an incandescent lamp with equivalent light output. However, they are unlikely to be economical when used only occasionally.

High-pressure sodium lamps

The high-pressure sodium (SON) lamp with its orange-yellow colour and poor colour rendering should be distinguished from the low-pressure sodium lamp (SOX) which gives out only yellow light so that everything illuminated by it can only look a particular shade of yellow, or black. In practice familiar scenes do not look quite as bad as that, since we know that pillar boxes are red and leaves green which influences our perception of them. Nevertheless, the effect of SOX lamps on coloured objects is quite awful and although in the past these lamps were widely used for highway lighting new installations are now rare as they have been largely replaced by the high-pressure type.

'Improved' or 'de luxe' types of high-pressure sodium lamp were the first of the large discharge sources to combine high efficacy and long life with a colour rendering index (Ra) of 50–60. Although their output is deficient in green they are considered suitable for railway stations, warehouses and so forth, while they have been extensively used for floodlighting, especially of red brick buildings. They have also been installed in some churches, especially those of red brick where their high light output and long life were thought to justify their barely acceptable colour rendering.

There has been intensive development of versions of the high-pressure sodium lamp with improved colour rendering, but the position is complicated by the fact that different manufacturers are pursuing rather different policies, and adopting different codings: such as SONDL, white SON and SDX. Many of these have Ra > 60 and the best are up to 82–83 and further improvements may be expected in the future. In general, the better the colour rendering the lower the light output.

It is not wise to mix lamps from different manufacturers.

- Even if they have similar colour rendering indices, they may not look the same.
- Lamps of the same manufacture but different wattage may also differ in colour.
- Again, site trials are likely to be necessary.

Typically, high-pressure sodium lamps with Ra > 80 suitable for church interior lighting are available in wattages from 35 up to 250 with lives of 6,000 hours burning or more. All have relatively low correlated colour temperatures (2,200 – 2,700°) and where a cooler light is required metal halide lamps are likely to be used. Lamps of higher wattage are available, but are probably more powerful than is likely to be desirable in a church, although they would be used for floodlighting.

High-pressure sodium lamps have the following properties:

- they require control gear and take some time to strike and run up when first switched on;
- if switched off they normally have to be allowed to cool before they will strike again;

- equipment is available which can ensure rapid restart if required;
- some can be dimmed if special arrangements are made, but this may involve complications.

Metal halide lamps

Metal halide lamps are the most recent of the 'high technology' sources and are still undergoing rapid development. There is intense competition between different manufacturers, who tend to use different trade terms and codes so that direct comparison is sometimes difficult. As with high-pressure sodium lamps, there is a trade-off between good colour rendering and high light output.

The best of the metal halide lamps has Ra > 90, unequalled by any other discharge type, but these are of high colour temperature and intended for films and sports stadia. Lamps suitable for use inside churches have Ra values of 80 to 85 with colour temperatures ranging from 3,000° to 4,200°, available in wattages from 35 up to 250.

Like all discharge lamps, metal halide types:

- require control gear;
- take time to run up to temperature when first switched on;
- will be difficult to restart within a short time of switching off;
- some can be dimmed if special gear is used, but at present only down to 30% of full output, not to extinction;
- the colour may alter both during run-up and dimming.

A type of metal halide lamp using a ceramic discharge tube, called CDM is smaller than others of similar wattage and its colour is more stable. It can therefore be used in smaller and neater fittings (luminaires) and a reflector version is also available which is very compact indeed.

Manufacturers are continually extending the range and improving the performance of metal halide lamps, so the information given above may soon become out of date.

Induction lamps

Nearly all high intensity discharge lamps have an inner *arc tube*, often of quartz glass or other special material which contains the electrodes and the chemicals through which the arc is passed. The wires connecting the electrodes to the supply have to pass through the walls of the arc tube and this always creates a potential weakness since it is very difficult to ensure a perfect seal throughout the range of temperatures that are likely to be experienced. Failures of these seals are the most important limitation on the life of discharge lamps.

The *induction lamp* avoids these problems by having no direct electrical connection between the electrodes and the supply. Instead the voltage between the electrodes is produced by *electromagnetic induction* – the transmission of energy through space using the same principle as the *induction loops* for hearing aids in churches and other auditoria, although in this case transmitting much greater power over very small distances. The 'transmitter' forms part of the lamp base and the 'receiver' is the sealed glass bulb itself.

The avoidance of weak points in construction makes it possible to design induction lamps with extremely long lives – one type is stated to have only 20% failures after 60,000 hours (nearly seven years of continuous burning) while there is an induction-type reflector spotlight with a life of 10,000 hours. Unfortunately they take some time to run up to full intensity and cannot be dimmed.

The range of induction lamps currently available is very limited but will doubtless increase in the future. At present their chief application for churches might be for lighting of spires, etc. where a crane or 'cherry picker' has to be brought in to change lamps, which is scarcely affordable on a two- or three-year basis. However, with floodlighting in use for 2,000 hours a year, a lamp with a nominal 60,000-hour life should last at least 20 years, which may well be acceptable.

Light emitting diodes (LEDs)

These are essentially semiconductors which emit light when a voltage is applied to them. Used singly they are well known as miniature indicator lamps for all kinds of electrical appliances, including socket outlets, etc. They are normally available in blue, red, green and yellow. They have very long lives, and at the time of writing, efforts are being made to use arrays of them as practical light sources, but so far their main application has been for signs and signals such as traffic lights. None of those that are currently available is likely to have much application in churches, with the possible exception of illuminated signs, but useful developments may be expected in the future.

The economics of different light sources

In comparing the economics of one type of light source with another the following factors must be taken into account:

- capital cost, best expressed as interest charges plus, where appropriate, a sinking fund for replacement;
- electricity cost per annum;
- maintenance cost per annum, including lamp replacement, cleaning, etc.

Only capital cost is independent of hours of use per annum, and assuming that an installation will last for 15 years, that the capital is charged at, say, 9% per annum and that where a sinking fund for replacement is needed it will cost a similar sum, the overall capital charges will come to 18% per annum. Churches which cover much of their capital expenditure by appeal may not always allow for capital charges in their accounting methods. If capital charges are ignored the system with the lowest running cost will then always be chosen, although it may not be the best value for money overall.

The cost of electricity per annum will, to a first approximation, be proportional to the hours of use. However, where there is a charge for maximum load in addition to one for each unit consumed, this may be only partly true, although most churches are likely to be paying for lighting on a flat rate per unit of electricity.

The annual cost of lamp replacement will depend on the hours of usage, the lamp life and the cost of access, in addition to the cost of the lamps themselves. For most churches it seems likely that the lighting system is cleaned only as lamps are replaced, and cost of cleaning will hardly appear as a separate charge. Where access is difficult the cost of bringing ladders or towers into the building to change lamps may be a significant item.

It is hard to make general comments about the relative capital cost of systems employing, say, incandescent and high-pressure sodium lamps without knowing how each is to be used. Discussion of 'typical' ways in which each source might be used is deferred until Chapters 5 and 6; nevertheless, the capital cost of each discharge lamp including housing and control gear is likely to be several times greater than that of a housing for an incandescent lamp, as against which many more incandescent lamps will be needed for equivalent light output.

Overall it would be expected that the capital cost of an installation employing discharge lamps is likely to be greater than that of one using incandescent lamps, *except where the incandescent option includes elaborate brass or crystal chandeliers*. However, for reasons to be explained in Chapters 5 and 6, it is unlikely that chandeliers used alone will be found satisfactory for present-day church lighting and in most cases we would expect the capital cost of an installation employing discharge lamps to exceed that of one employing incandescent lamps alone.

In comparing the overall economics of discharge lighting as against incandescent lighting for a church we are likely to find that the former has higher capital charges and the latter higher running cost per hour's use. It follows that the more hours per annum the lighting is in use, the more likely it is that the installation cost of discharge lighting will be justified.

To give a specific example, suppose that for a particular building discharge lighting will cost £2,000 more than incandescent lighting initially, but save 20p per hour in electricity costs. The cost of lamp replacement is more difficult to assess, firstly because the price of discharge lamps varies markedly from one supplier to another, and secondly because where the lamps can be changed by the verger or a member of the congregation without charge, the cost is only that of the lamp itself.

The simplest assumption is that the cost of lamp changing will be the same for both kinds of source: each discharge lamp might cost, say, 20 times as much as an incandescent lamp, but there may be only half as many and each will last 10 times as long.

On these assumptions:
- £2,000, notionally costing 18%, that is £360 per annum, has been spent to save 20p per hour.
- If the lighting is in use for 1,800 hours per annum the two systems break even.
- For more than 1,800 hours use per annum discharge lighting is cheaper overall.

- For less than 1,800 hours use per annum incandescent lighting is cheaper overall.

The calculation can be repeated for any other figures and for different interest rates and so on.

In many country churches the annual hours of use of the lighting are little more than 200, no more than an average of 4 hours per week throughout the year, but in others, especially in towns, the usage may be much greater. It is worth noting that for industry, street lighting and so forth, where discharge lighting is mainly used, the annual hours of usage may be substantially in excess of 2,000, and for street lighting on all night it is 4,500 hours per annum.

Where churches are floodlit from dusk to 11 p.m. daily the annual hours of usage of the floodlighting are about 1,600 and if kept on until midnight annual usage will be nearly 2,000 hours. Discharge lighting will then always be the more economical.

By contrast, suppose that the cost of lamp changing is not the same for both systems. We may still assume that the cost of the lamps themselves will be much the same, but if a contractor has to be employed to change lamps at high level the economics are transformed. Suppose the contractor charges £200 for his work, in addition to the cost of lamps, and that the lighting is in use for 500 hours per annum. Incandescent lamps must be changed every two years (that is, £100 per annum to the contractor), but discharge lamps only every 10 years (£20 per annum to the contractor).

The figures are now as follows:
- Every year discharge lamps involve an extra £180 in capital charges, but for 500 hours usage save £100 in electricity and £80 in the cost of lamp changing – they break even.
- If the annual usage exceeds 500 hours discharge lamps apparently save money.
- However, this calculation is rather unrealistic since it seems unlikely that the lamps and fittings could be left without cleaning for as long as ten years.
- Nevertheless, it does explain the apparent attraction of discharge sources, even those of only moderate colour rendering, for certain churches.

With the generally improved colour rendering of some discharge sources plus the use of dimmers to extend the life of incandescent lamps, the dilemma of cost versus colour quality should not nowadays appear in quite the same form as it did only ten years ago. The issues involved are discussed in Chapters 7 and 8.

Comparison of possible light sources

Type of source	Light output (in lumen/watt) (see Appendix 1)	Typical rated life (in hours)	External ctrl gear	Typical colour temp (in °K) (see Appendix 3)	CRI (Ra) (max value 100) (See Appendix 3)	Price of lamp only (a very rough guide)	Wattage range (sizes suitable for churches)	Main snags
INCANDESCENT								
GLS	10	1,000	No	2,700	90+	Low	15–300	Heat output
Reflector spot	10	1,000	No	2,700	90+	Fairly low	30–100	Life unreliable
PAR 38 Reflector	10	2,000	No	2,700	90+	Fairly low	75–150	Few when used correctly
TUNGSTEN-HALOGEN								
PAR 30/38 type	15	2,000–3,000	No	3,000	90+	Medium	30–100	Cost
Linear	16	2,000	No	3,000	90+	Low	100–750	Risk of glare
LOW VOLTAGE								
Min. reflector	18	2,500	Transformer	3,000	90+	Medium	20–75	Needs special dimmer
LINEAR FLUORESCENT								
Tri-phosphor	85	12,000	Yes	2,700–6,000	80+	Medium	18–100	Long and difficult to conceal
Standard	40–70	7,500	Yes	2,700–6,000	50–75	Low/medium	4–85	Long and difficult to conceal
COMPACT FLUORESCENT (CFLs)								
Used with external gear	40+	10,000	Yes	2,700–4,000	80+	Medium	5–55	Only some dimmable
Fitted with internal gear	50+	10,000	No	2,700–4,000	80+	High	7–25	Only some dimmable
HIGH-PRESSURE SODIUM								
'Improved'	80	12,000	Yes	2,200	50–55	High	50–250	Dimming not recommended, colour marginal
'White SON'	45	10,000	Yes	2,500	80+	High	35–100	Dimming not recommended
METAL HALIDE INCLUDING CDM								
Smaller sizes	75+	6,000+	Yes	3,000–4,000	80+	High	35–150	Dimming not recommended
(Further developments expected)								
INDUCTION								
Limited range (2000)	45+	10,000–60,000	Varies	2,700–4,000	80+	High	23–85	Limited range

chapter 5
Lighting fittings (luminaires)

The technical term for a lighting fitting is 'luminaire'. This includes all the equipment necessary to connect the electricity supply to the lamp. The colloquial term 'fitting' is used in this guide as it is the more common usage in the UK. In the USA the term 'lighting fixture' is used.

Fittings can vary from a simple lamp socket to a highly complex assembly of electronic and mechanical components. While the fitting must, as a minimum, hold the lamp securely, provide an electrical connection and dissipate the heat generated by the lamp and control gear so that both can operate at an acceptable temperature, it may also:

- protect the lamp from dust and possibly water, mechanical damage, or a hostile environment, which is particularly important in the case of external lighting;
- accommodate the control gear needed by discharge lamps, or the transformer required by extra low voltage lamps, although both of these can be separate items;
- project the light from the lamp in one or more particular directions;
- provide a shield to prevent glare or a diffuser to render the directly emitted light less concentrated;
- form a decorative element, in which case the fitting can become more important in its own right than the light it emits;
- disguise the origin of the light and merge into the background.

It is not commonly appreciated that the fitting can absorb a large percentage (30–60%) of the light emitted by the lamp.

Manufacturers often classify fittings by terms such as 'decorative', 'commercial', or 'display', but such terms are misleading, and in the context of churches the difference lies between those which are intended to be part of the visible furnishing of the church and those which are intended to be inconspicuous or even concealed.

Most modern light sources are too bright to be viewed comfortably in normal conditions by the naked eye and the fitting has to remedy this. Visible fittings may do so by diffusers which increase the size of the visible light source and so reduce it to an acceptable brightness, becoming in the process a major design element. Design of fittings is increasingly concerned with directing the light produced by the lamp in predictable directions with predictable intensity. If a diffuser is not provided such fittings must be installed in positions where the lamp is outside the normal line of sight, or shielded from direct view, in order to avoid glare and discomfort.

Interior fittings

Floor standing Early torchères and candelabra became very decorative, and nowadays such fittings are frequently used to provide uplighting, a form of indirect lighting in which the light is first directed at the ceiling and upper walls and is received at lower level only after reflection. The ability to move a floor standard about can be an advantage, but it is important to take care with the flexible lead.

Wall brackets Brackets are frequently used to provide uplighting (see above), but even when an asymmetrical reflector is used to project the light away from the wall there is usually a flash of bright light above the fitting. A site trial is desirable before permanent wiring is installed both to assess effects of this kind, and also to check whether fortuitous harsh shadows are generated or defects in the wall surface emphasized. In many buildings it is difficult to take the electrical supply to wall brackets without defacing the wall.

Pendants Before the popularity of fittings with reflectors most churches were lit by pendants hanging at a relatively low level. There are few such products available today which either look or perform well in older churches. Conversion or upgrading the often beautiful historic fittings is discussed on pages 36–7. Pendant lighting can sometimes provide both architectural emphasis and useful light, as with a corona over an altar resited in a crossing, but it must never be allowed either to obscure important features or to clutter up the space (often called 'space pollution'). Pendants are often installed in positions which present problems for relamping and cleaning, while integrating both fitting and suspension points with the architecture of the building can be difficult. In particular, suspension from the soffit of a nave/aisle arcade is generally unsatisfactory both aesthetically and as regards light distribution.

Ceiling-mounted fittings These are not normally expected to be conspicuous in themselves but use the ceiling as the most convenient location from which to project the light. Whether recessed or surface mounted, their positions must be carefully integrated with the architecture since they are usually visible. In most cases louvres are needed to prevent glare. If these fittings are not designed to emit some light upward and sideways onto the surface on which they are fixed, other lighting may be needed to provide illumination on the ceiling to avoid the sense of gloom associated with a dark ceiling, called the 'tunnel effect'. Ceiling-mounted fittings are frequently used under galleries where there is insufficient headroom or no suitable location for other types. Access for maintenance where ceilings are high can be a problem unless there is an accessible roof void.

Projectors There is no generally accepted name for the large variety of fittings now available for indoor use, which were designed primarily for display purposes, but are often used for church lighting. The terms 'floodlight' and 'spotlight' are commonly employed; basically both terms describe a fitting in which the light is directed in a cone in a particular direction by a reflector and sometimes by a lens as well. In the 'floodlight' the emission of light is over a wide angle from the fitting, thus 'flooding' the scene with light. In the spotlight, light is emitted in a relatively narrow cone and can be concentrated on a particular object or group of objects. Many 'floodlights' exert little control over the light emitted, and can be a serious source of glare because the lamp can be seen from a wide area of the scene lit. Both floodlights and spotlights are apt to create harsh contrasts.

Fibre optics   These are not in fact a type of fitting, but the term describes a recent development where the light from a lamp in a closed housing is concentrated through a flexible bundle of glass or plastic fibres and emitted at the far end. Normally several fibre bundles are connected to a single light box. The light emitted at the end of the fibre bundle is normally passed through a lens to restrict or spread it. The advantages of such equipment are first that the light from a single lamp in an accessible position can be taken to several positions which are not themselves readily accessible for maintenance, and second that no heat or ultraviolet radiation is passed through the fibre bundle. This makes fibre optics particularly suitable for lighting delicate and fugitive materials (see Chapter 9). The disadvantages are that the heat from the inevitably high-powered lamp has to be dissipated, usually by a fan which emits noise, and that typically only a quarter of the light emitted by the lamp reaches the lighted objects. The equipment is expensive, but can be worthwhile where the installation of a large number of small lights in a relatively small area is required, for instance for choir stalls.

Exterior fittings

Bollards   These external fittings are a development from the traffic bollard, generally designed to light an area of ground around the fitting. The light is directed downwards which can be unsatisfactory, for instance at the top of a flight of steps, and bollards can be intrusive in the landscape. Vandalism can also be a problem unless they are very strongly constructed.

Brackets   These are traditionally used externally as a convenient way of fixing a light to a building where the electrical supply can easily be run to it, and are normally designed to give all-round light. It is undesirable to allow much light to rise uncontrolled above the level of the fitting.

Floodlights   This is the common term for lights intended to illuminate an area of ground or the exterior of a building rather than the traffic routes around it. Floodlights incorporate reflectors and sometimes lenses, and it is important to ensure that an appropriate combination is used to fulfil the precise lighting requirement. Glare from badly directed or unsuitably sited floodlights is a common cause of complaint, and they can be a source of other forms of 'light pollution'. If accessible, these fittings are liable to vandalism or theft (see Chapter 6). The front glass of these fittings always becomes hot, often dangerously so.

Buried uplighters   These are a form of floodlight in which the lamp is housed in a watertight container and buried below ground level, with a flush cover glass. The light may be directed at a wall by using an asymmetric reflector and louvres, and devices to prevent damage are available. These fittings always produce a bright patch near the base of a wall and should only be used where this is acceptable architecturally. They also tend to emphasize horizontal projections and wall textures. There is a tendency for the container to leak, and the cover glass always becomes very hot. Nearly all those on the market are designed for exterior use, which is why they are included here, but they are sometimes used indoors as well.

Security lights The purpose of these fittings is to deter possible intruders or vandals, and small units spreading the light over a wide area fitted with lamps of high power which glare are normally used. After dark, on the approach of a moving body an infra-red presence detector (PIR, see Chapter 7) switches on the light for a relatively short but adjustable period. The PIR may be incorporated into the fitting or located at a distance, and it can operate several lights. The wiring to these fittings should be run so that it cannot easily be broken by an intruder, while the fittings themselves should be located out of easy reach. A master switch to prevent intermittent operation during a service may be needed.

Lamp standards A standard or column is a device for mounting a fitting in an isolated position some distance above ground level and, as noted for external brackets, it is undesirable to allow much light to be emitted in an uncontrolled way above the horizontal. The electrical supply is normally brought into the column below ground and rises internally to the light fitting proper, often termed a lantern. Lanterns can incorporate floodlighting as well as lighting for the surrounding ground, but the floodlighting element is likely to be limited even when specially designed. While extra height deters vandalism, maintenance may be a problem, and high columns can appear out of scale with surrounding buildings.

'Decorative' fittings

This section is concerned with those fittings which have been selected primarily to provide visual embellishment to the building, irrespective of their light output, although this can often provide a useful component of the total lighting.

The most common decorative fittings are historic chandeliers originally designed to burn candles or gas and perhaps already converted to use tungsten lamps. They were intended to provide the standard of lighting expected at the time of their manufacture, which is much less than that of today. The problem is how to refurbish them and improve their performance when their total electrical load may already be high and the power of the lamp cannot be increased without creating intolerable glare, quite apart from the risk of exceeding permissible limits for heat and electrical load. In a church where there is high reflectance from the walls and ceiling these fittings may possibly be capable of producing the general light required, provided that consideration is given to controlling glare. In practice, as the source of light is visible, it is probably too bright for comfort.

The appearance of a chandelier is important from the viewpoint not only of the congregation, but also of the pulpit which may be raised above floor level and have a different background against which the light is seen. As explained above, in most churches chandeliers are unlikely to provide adequate light by themselves, and it is necessary to decide whether or not to fit lamps of relatively low wattage purely to give the fittings life and perhaps sparkle, retaining them mainly for their decorative effect and to assist in softening shadows from other directional sources.

Sparkle is related to glare, but whereas the latter hinders clear vision, sparkle in the form of a myriad of points of bright light can give visual pleasure without interfering with accurate vision, and this is the design principle behind the crystal chandelier. Sparkle can be provided by shining a high intensity spotlight from a remote position onto a brass chandelier, but the shadows must fall where they are not distracting. With a complex chandelier it is often possible to incorporate additional but inconspicuous projectors to ensure that enough light is emitted in the direction in which it is needed (*see figure 5*).

While the electrical and lighting characteristics of new chandeliers can be satisfactory, they should not be accepted for existing buildings without ensuring that their scale is suitable. Fittings purchased on the basis of illustrations in catalogues may not necessarily be so, and the best way to assess them is to suspend a mock-up in the building.

It is not usually satisfactory to replace visible tungsten lamps in any fitting with compact fluorescent lamps (CFLs, see Chapter 4). Not only is the lamp size and light output different, but the appearance of the casing, often milk-white, may be unacceptable. These lamps kill sparkle and if used in a brass chandelier can make it appear lifeless, even if they are not actually visible. Bare tubular CFLs have been used as 'candles' in refits: even if the background is not so dark that glare is produced it is very much a matter of opinion whether they are acceptable in this situation.

Inconspicuous fittings

Some fittings are often camouflaged to merge into the background against which they are seen, or hidden behind architectural features. The heat generated by a fitting may be a problem when it is concealed. Not only does the whole fitting produce heat which must be allowed to dissipate, but the beam of light can be sufficiently hot to ignite flammable materials nearby and manufacturers normally advise the safe distance, either on a plate fixed to the fitting or in a leaflet packed with it. This is important when tucking fittings into recesses containing flammable materials. Even if the materials are not flammable, the continual expansion and contraction due to heating and cooling as the lamp is switched on and off may lead to cracking and other damage in the long term.

There is a tendency with all fittings, particularly if they are ventilated by convection, for stray light to emerge in unexpected directions or be reflected from unexpected surfaces, and this can only be checked by site testing. 'Concealed' fittings often betray their presence in this way, but this may be of benefit by demonstrating that the lamp is still working. If light from concealed fittings is reflected too brightly from adjacent surfaces it can be corrected by adjusting the angle, painting the surface in a less reflective colour, or more normally by a baffle.

Illustrations in manufacturers' literature can give a misleading idea of the size of a fitting and a sample should be offered up in situ. Concealed fittings using linear fluorescent tubes have to be manoeuvred into position and it is necessary to check that this is possible and that relamping can be carried

fig. 5
Electrified candelabra at Ely Cathedral.

Photographs © McCloud & Co. Ltd.

Electrification by McCloud & Co. Ltd.

out. It is also necessary to check that 'adjustable' fittings can be adjusted and locked to the required position when mounted as planned.

The colour of most standard fittings is normally limited, generally to black or white plus sometimes chrome, anodised aluminium, or brass (satin or polished). Where camouflage is important most manufacturers will supply to a special colour, but at a price and often only for a significant quantity. This delays delivery and makes later changes more difficult. If a fitting is not itself illuminated from another one, it is not always necessary to be too precise about colour matching. For small numbers heat-resistant spray paint may be used on site. In general, polished metallic finishes are to be avoided as they are likely to draw attention to the fitting by reflecting light from other sources or even from the sun.

Specially designed fittings

Purpose-made fittings are expensive, but the cost may be justified if the result is a layout or the use of a light source that is more economical in capital or running cost than its alternatives. In sensitive historic locations a 'special' may be the only acceptable fitting, and any chandelier used for more than decorative reasons and not completely purpose designed must at least be modified. A manufacturer's standard product may perform satisfactorily, but if modified may no longer be guaranteed. For this reason a prototype must always be tested on site since the performance of purpose-made fittings is sometimes a great disappointment. Nevertheless there are firms well known for their 'specials', and in many cases their expertise justifies their reputation.

General points

Fittings are often very heavy, and must be provided with secure fixings. In general, brass or stainless steel screws and plastic plugs (not drilled into historic masonry but into the mortar joints) should be used. Many fittings are sold for use with lighting tracks, which are metal or plastic channels with continuous internal electrical contacts on which fittings may be mounted and connected at any position, subject to overall limits of weight and electrical loading. The ability of the track to support the weight proposed should be checked, particularly if fixed to a vertical surface. Track fixing is really only suitable if a large number of fittings are to be mounted in a line over a short distance, or if flexibility is truly required by the brief.

No fitting with an unenclosed reflector should be mounted in an accessible position in a church, because of the danger of people accidentally touching the hot lamp. This is particularly important with equipment employing tungsten-halogen lamps, which run extremely hot, and even when mounted out of normal reach should be fitted with some form of protective cover which cannot be removed without the use of tools.

It is not usual for uplighters using fluorescent lamps to be provided with a cover glass as a standard item, but this should be added to prevent the collection of dead insects. All uplighters must be capable of being dusted easily.

In churches which are intermittently heated (as most are) there may at times be condensation on cold metal surfaces which is highly corrosive, and a protective coating is necessary. Protection should also be given from electrolytic corrosion due to contact between dissimilar metals.

chapter 6
Design

The considerations affecting the design of interior lighting are basically different from those for exterior lighting and will be treated separately.

Interior lighting

By day churches receive natural light which, in the case of recent buildings, was planned by the designer or, in the case of historic buildings, was limited by the structural techniques of the day and may have been modified by subsequent users. If the daylight in a building is unsatisfactory it can sometimes be improved, subject to statutory permission, by increasing or decreasing the amount of daylight permitted to enter.

Daylight itself, however, is subject to wide variations in intensity and direction, and while historic buildings were, in general, designed to be seen in daylight, the requirements of modern use may mean that the natural light has to be supplemented. In doing this it is necessary to ensure that the added light does not distort the appearance of the building by emphasizing inappropriate features or introducing unacceptable colour contrasts with natural light. In particular, sources used primarily during the day, especially where they may be seen during sunshine, should preferably have a 'cool' appearance, that is one of high colour temperature, in place of the warmer colours generally preferred at night.

There is another fundamental difference between supplementary lighting in daytime and lighting for use at night, since with the latter there are opportunities for creating emphases quite different from those in the building by day. This freedom should not transcend the main purpose of the church, which is to house the congregation and focus their minds on the liturgy in a sympathetic environment. The most beautiful ceiling, the most impressive monuments, should not be emphasized to a point at which they attract attention to the detriment of the liturgy. A church is not a museum.

Determinants

The lighting design must start by establishing the environment in which the congregation wish to worship, and this has varied in the past between the extremes illustrated by a seventeenth-century preaching house and a nineteenth-century Tractarian church: nowadays it will differ for Anglo-Catholic and evangelical/charismatic congregations.

The next consideration is the building itself, and the lighting must not merely provide unobtrusive or decorative sources but also respond to the structural form and style, avoiding disruptive shadows or unintended bright patches (*see figure 6*). For instance, a Gothic building usually has clearly defined structural sub-divisions, and installing lighting which ignores them will generally appear jarring and discordant. Careful consideration of the merits of the individual church and of the attributes which make it unique should allow the design to reveal them while still respecting the main

Design

fig. 6
Badly chosen and sited downlighters (note the unwanted and disagreeable patterns on the wall).

Photograph © Bill Crawforth

considerations of use and focus, much as a rich background can enhance a tapestry. Such an analysis may also suggest the possibility of embellishing with light what might otherwise be a relatively uninteresting environment.

As explained in Chapter 2, objects which are lighted significantly more brightly than their surroundings attract attention. For this reason the position at which the most important part of the liturgy is taking place at any time should receive preferential lighting. These places are principally the altar, pulpit, lectern, font and chancel steps. The illuminances recommended in Appendix 1 assume night-time use. By day overall levels may be considerably higher, and to add emphasis at any position may need considerably stronger lighting than would be necessary at night.

Illuminance

The amount of light normally considered sufficient to enable the congregation to read comfortably in a church is considerably lower than that normally provided for reading in other types of building, such as schools or offices. This helps not only to generate a sense of tranquillity but also to assist in creating a hierarchy of lighting levels, focusing on the liturgy. Stronger lighting is needed for those reading music and at the lectern, and the needs

41

of members of the congregation with poor eyesight can be met by ensuring that some seating in the nave has brighter lighting than elsewhere. However, people who have sat in one pew for many years are often unwilling to move merely because their eyesight deteriorates, and this may create problems. While some variation in the lighting of the nave can be attractive, the creation of conspicuous pools of bright light should be avoided.

Installations should be flexible, and the designer must consider the effect which will result if part rather than the whole is in use. Various means of control are described in Chapter 7, and the necessity for the parish to consider the extent to which they need flexibility is emphasized in Chapter 3.

Balance and spill light

When providing light for a specific section of the church it is inevitable that a certain amount, generally called spill light, will illuminate other areas as well. While this is often desirable, care should be taken that it is not overdone. Pews lit to 100 lux are necessary, whereas nave walls lit to the same level will be too bright, unless of dark stone or brick, but far too often fittings are installed which spread light indiscriminately over both surfaces.

In a typical Gothic church which consists at least of a nave and a clearly defined chancel, the chancel walls should be brighter than those of the nave, and the altar and reredos brighter still, framed by the chancel arch with an intermediate level of brightness. In a church which does not have these spatial separations, for instance a typical Georgian church, the walls surrounding the sanctuary should be rather brighter than elsewhere.

In general, an over-bright roof, however beautiful or richly carved, is inappropriate in a Gothic building, but a totally dark roof space is depressing and should be avoided. In a church where the walls and ceiling are light in colour and the whole environment is lighter, the ceiling may well be the primary illuminated surface. In favourable circumstances this can provide sufficient general illumination by reflection (indirect or uplighting), relying on additional lighting only to emphasize important elements.

With the relatively low light levels common in churches, even lighting must be avoided as it tends to produce an impression of dullness and even gloom. However, excessive contrast, for instance by relying largely on the use of narrow beam spotlights, may appear stagey, while illogical variations in brightness merely disrupt the environment, drawing attention to things which should not be prominent. Care and balance are always necessary.

Emphasis

The perceived brightness of an object depends not only on the amount of light it reflects, but also on how it compares with the background against which it is seen. This is important not only when considering lighting an altar frontal or reredos but also in considering a painted chancel compared with a panelled one, or the effect of a chandelier in an interior decorated in light colours as compared with one having exposed brick walls and timber roof. Gentle emphasis of aesthetically admirable, even if liturgically unimportant, elements such as a fine statue or carved ornament can enrich the environment without detracting from the proper focus of attention, and dispel any sense of gloom.

Modelling

As explained in Chapter 2, contrasts of light and shade are an important element in design. The shadows thrown by an arcade or roof timbers – lighted objects seen against a darker background – texture revealed by light grazing a surface, all enrich the environment. This presupposes a dominant direction in the lighting, which cannot, in general, be achieved if several sources spread around the church emit light equally in all directions as, for instance, where lighting is principally by pendants with diffusers.

Daylight is usually brighter from the south, and where choice exists the strength of artificial light should follow the same pattern. Light entirely from one direction will tend to cast dark shadows which should be softened by a weaker light from the opposing direction. Where internal surfaces are generally light in colour enough light for this purpose may be obtained by inter-reflection, and the soft ambient light from pendants may also perform the same function.

Modelling is critically important for the human face, whose visibility is necessary for full communication, and the lighting of the clergy at the altar, at the chancel steps, and particularly at the pulpit, requires special attention (*see figure 2*).

Glare

Appendix 2 includes a detailed discussion of glare. It is obvious that light sources which are too bright should be avoided, especially if seen against a dark background when they may dazzle the viewer. Bright sources should generally be located outside the normal direction of view, but it is often difficult to manage this at the altar and on the chancel steps. However, glare must be avoided for clergy at the pulpit since it is important that they can see the congregation without straining.

Attempts to increase the light output of existing fittings, particularly pendants and chandeliers, by increasing lamp power beyond that for which they were designed may result in glare so that the words and music can no longer be read in comfort. The same effect can occur when a large east window is so bright that the altar cannot be seen properly.

Special features

Altars Elements or activities which need to be emphasized require dedicated supplementary lighting. Of these the most important is the altar, which may have a decorative embroidered frontal and carry a brass or silver cross. While the altar generally should be more brightly lit than its setting, care has to be exercised to avoid distracting shadows of officiating clergy falling on the walls or other visible surfaces.

Altar frontals and furniture Frontals should be lit to the same level as the clergy officiating at the altar during a service, but if they have historical value they should be covered for protection from light at other times (see Chapter 9). The light should be directed to reveal the texture of the material, and the colour rendering of the source may be important, particularly because it may change the appearance of one colour in relation to another. A trial of the proposed source, made after the installation of the general lighting, on all the frontals used throughout the Church's year may be revealing, and will also show up any problems which might arise if a light source differing from that of the ambient lighting is proposed.

Metallic finishes are usual in both frontals and reredoses, but they will not be apparent if the light falling on them is not reflected directly towards the viewer. This will not be a problem with raised patterns, but flat areas with a metallic finish can virtually disappear and ruin the appearance. **It is not always realized that altar furniture, particularly crosses with flat metal faces, can present the same problem, and their shadows on a rear wall may appear more solid than the objects themselves, while flat polished surfaces can sometimes cast unwanted reflections on the walls** (*see figure 7*).

fig. 7
Inappropriate lighting obscuring the details of altar furniture and casting unwanted shadows.

Photograph © Bill Crawforth

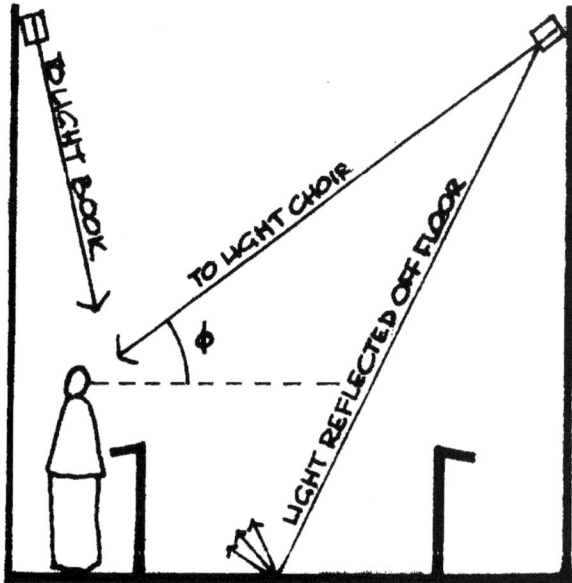

fig. 8
Lighting of the choristers' faces and music.

Light on the faces must come from in front, light for the music must come from over the shoulders.

© Bill Crawforth

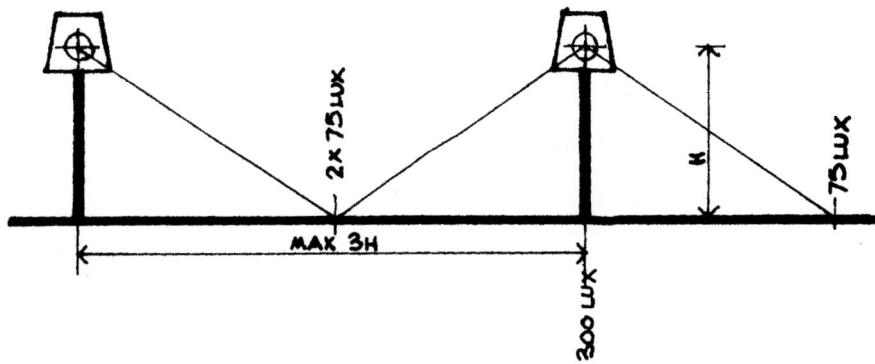

fig. 9

Lighting the choir from standards.

Spacing of standards should not be more than three times their height above the desk.

© Bill Crawforth

Choir stalls These are generally best lit with the main light falling onto the score over the shoulders of the choir and secondary light on their faces (*see figure 8*). Stall-mounted lights may be aesthetically attractive and, if well designed, can provide the high level of light needed by the choir plus sparkle and colour without competing with the appearance of the altar.

Stall-mounted fittings should be tall enough to illuminate the score both when it is on the book rest and when held in the hand and must be spaced at intervals not greater than three times their height (see figure 9). They must be shaded to prevent glare both for the singer and congregation, and must also be safe against tampering by the choir. **When the implications of all these requirements are thoroughly understood the attractions of standards mounted on the stalls may appear less compelling than is often thought.**

The use of low-voltage lamps or optic-fibre lighting are possible ways of ensuring safety. The most successful designs usually incorporate two lamps, a visible one of low power giving gentle ambient lighting (even candles may be sufficient), the other concealed with a brighter light directed onto the score. Choirs are particularly susceptible to glare from badly located light sources in the body of the church which can render the score illegible if the singer happens to look up. Organists should be able to see the choir clearly from the console, and care has to be taken to protect them from the same problem.

Lecterns and pulpits The lectern is best furnished with a switched or dimmable reading lamp above the book rest, but where this is not possible (for instance with a valuable antique lectern) a concealed spotlight from above shining onto the book is possible. The pulpit has similar requirements, but, in addition, the preacher's face must be clearly visible. There is a danger that grotesque shadows will be thrown by spotlights directed at the preacher, and the wall behind the pulpit should receive some light from a different source to minimize this risk. Further, if the upward light from the reading lamp is not counteracted by light from a more natural angle, the appearance of the preacher's face will be most unpleasant (*see figures 2b and 2e*). However, any spotlight directed at the preacher's face must be well outside the normal direction of view when looking at the congregation, to avoid distraction and glare.

Rood screens and reredoses Rood screens, with or without a rood, sometimes separate the chancel from the nave of a church, and they are frequently major works of art in their own right. They have no liturgical function, but are nevertheless dominant visual elements. Where the altar

fig. 10
Lighting a reredos.

Photographs © Bill Crawforth

(*a*) clumsily lit from below

(*b*) the same reredos where the modelling has been well displayed by careful lighting

remains in its traditional position to the east of the screen the latter can present a visual barrier, and should not be illuminated during a service to the extent that it dominates the view of the chancel (unless, of course, the service is confined to the chancel). Where the altar has been brought forward, westward of the screen, the latter can form a reredos to the altar and be illuminated together with the chancel as a setting for the altar.

When the church is not in use for services but open to visitors the screen or reredos may be illuminated as a feature, either activated by the visitor on a timed basis, or permanently. This illumination should be of low intensity by comparison with the fully lighted church. The lighting should, of course, be designed to suit the characteristics of the screen, as indicated in the following paragraph (*see also figures 10 and 11*).

Monuments and works of art Roods, monuments, statues and pictures do not form part of the liturgy, but it may be desirable to illuminate them at

Design

fig. 11 Lighting a reredos.

Photographs © Bill Crawforth

(*a*) lighting carefully balanced from both sides

(*b*) the same with half the lighting showing an unbalanced appearance

other times, or as background decoration. The lighting of each object should be considered separately, to bring out its shape and texture, and also to fulfil the need for conservation by controlling both the amount of light and its infra-red and ultraviolet content, as discussed in Chapter 9. See also the Bibliography (Appendix 6).

Stained glass windows Large windows appear black at night and often mar the appearance of a church. Unless there is a reflective surface behind the window which can be flooded with light, little can be done about clear glass, but stained glass can be illuminated by external floodlights. The effect depends on the extent to which the light is diffused within the glass, and it requires very strong sources out of the line of sight of the congregation. Most of the light passes through the glass and casts a coloured image of the window on the surface on which it falls, while some of the remaining light is seen as illuminating the glass. The effect depends not only on the cleanliness and wear of the glass, but also on the internal brightness of the wall in which

47

the window is set. A metal halide lamp with good colour rendering is needed to bring out the range of colours usual in stained glass. Unfortunately the exterior of the window will also be very brightly illuminated, well above the normal level for external floodlighting, and the acceptability of the appearance from outside must be carefully considered.

Musical and dramatic performances

The performers usually occupy a position in the chancel or immediately to the west of the chancel arch, facing the nave. In all churches good lighting should have been provided for this area, and while, if separately and suitably controlled (see Chapter 7), it may be adequate for a small group, it will not normally be sufficient for choirs or dramatic performances. The extent to which permanent provision should be made for musical events depends on the frequency of such activities. As regards drama, it is unlikely that a permanent installation will serve any but the simplest presentation.

Lighting of musicians or singers on the chancel steps from the nave will not illuminate the scores, and where it is difficult to locate westward pointing fittings unobtrusively in the chancel, illuminated music stands may be a solution. A temporary gantry or acoustic reflector can also support fittings mounted overhead.

Dramatic performances often require elaborate lighting. One way of providing very basic facilities is to install accessible, inconspicuous three-circuit mains voltage tracks with dimming and switching on each circuit, into which interchangeable spotlights can be plugged at will or cleared away when not in use.

These measures will not meet the requirements of ambitious productions, for which specialist stage lighting equipment and a control board will be brought in. The latter should be fed from a heavy-duty connector box with cable entry provided for the purpose. This should be lockable and mastered by a suitable (60 A or more) fused switch or an adjacent circuit breaker. In new buildings it may be possible to provide permanent mountings to carry stage lighting equipment, but this is unlikely to be practicable in older buildings. A duct allowing temporary cables to be passed safely across the church from north to south near the chancel arch is a useful facility, to be installed when an opportunity presents itself.

Such a duct for temporary cables must be quite large since the cables will be fitted with plugs at one end and sockets at the other. A single 100 mm pipe will not be adequate, although a cluster of four or six such pipes might be of value. It will be possible to construct such a duct only in rather special circumstances, for instance if the chancel is to be raised, extended or provided with a new floor. If there is an accessible crypt below the chancel, a trap down to the crypt on both north and south sides may be a viable substitute for a duct.

Lighting techniques

A good design may employ a variety of lighting techniques and, as with the fittings themselves, there is a basic distinction between the use of visible light sources which form part of the church furnishings even when not in use, and the use of fittings intended to be inconspicuous or even invisible in themselves.

Uplighting or indirect lighting, in which light is projected upwards from inconspicuous sources to be reflected downwards onto the books and participants has the characteristic that the first reflecting surface, usually the ceiling, is the brightest surface in view. Further, the reflected light is diffuse and lacks the shadows required to assist in defining the shape of objects. Moreover, even with a light coloured ceiling a considerable proportion of the incident light is absorbed, so that the system can be rather wasteful.

Uplighting can successfully provide a gentle ambient light if combined with other forms of illumination that provide contrast for modelling, and there are situations when it is the only practicable way of lighting parts of a church, for instance the area under a low gallery.

Downlighting, in which all the light is directed downwards has the disadvantage of throwing harsh shadows (*see figure* 6) unless the floor and walls are unusually light in colour. Depending on the number and position of the sources, a very even and economic distribution of light on seating can be achieved, but the ceiling or roof space from which the lights are suspended or mounted remains dark with the risk of glare to those looking upwards. Supplementary light is needed to rectify this, and may also be needed to illuminate surrounding walls and to soften shadows. In historic ceilings there will also be objections to cutting holes for the fittings or connections.

Internal floodlighting means 'flooding' a space with broad beams of light of high power, which may produce a reasonably even level of light on all illuminated surfaces and, if there are many fittings and light-coloured decorations, soft shadows. This form is good for revealing the texture of surfaces over large areas and it can provide good background illumination, but with the dangers of glare described on page 43. The principle of ensuring a dominant direction of light, discussed above, can be met by this technique.

Spotlighting is the normal means of providing accent lighting for significant elements. If there is a reasonable amount of light reaching the object from other sources, increasing the intensity by a factor of about three over the surroundings by using one or more spotlights will provide suitable emphasis. If virtually all light comes from a single direction the effect may be harsh.

In lighting from a high level there is a potential conflict between the need for good modelling of faces and the avoidance of glare for people looking towards the fitting.

- For modelling the direction of illumination should not be too close to the vertical, otherwise the effect will be as in figure 2d, but to avoid glare the direction of the beam should be well away from the horizontal.
- An angle to the vertical between 30° and 45° will be a suitable compromise in most cases.
- This angle should be measured along the axis of the beam and not simply on a sectional drawing. In figure 12 the true direction of illumination is θ, whereas on a long section it will appear to be α, and on a short section β.

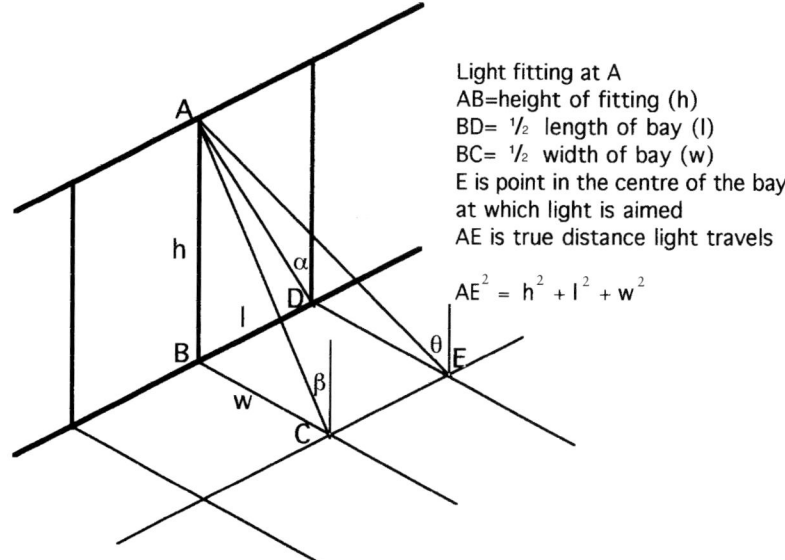

fig. 12
Measurement of the direction of a beam of light.
© Bill Crawforth

- Although spotlights emit the most powerful light at the centre of the beam they also give out a good deal over a wider range of angles. Unless great care is taken the edge of the beam may therefore give rise to glare.

Reflected light is present in any lit interior, but is usually less in a church than in most other buildings. The proportion of inter-reflected light (that is, light reflected between walls, ceiling and floor and back again, etc.) affects the basic character of the lighting and the choices which can be made. For example, chandeliers which would be sources of glare in a dark church may be perfectly satisfactory in one with light decorations. However, too high a proportion of inter-reflected light will tend to soften shadows and create a bland interior unless additional directional lighting is used to counteract the effect.

Computer programs written to aid lighting design generally assume a rectangular space with solid walls having simple reflective characteristics, and great care has to be exercised in applying them to more complex spaces such as churches. In particular, the assumptions made by the operator can distort the result: for instance the effect of light spilling through open arcades is difficult to handle on a computer, which usually regards the arcade as a solid wall, and the operator has to decide how reflective this theoretical wall may be, and how to deal with the light spilling into the adjacent space.

Site trials

Site trials of lighting are valuable design tools but if on too small a scale can be misleading. Trials can demonstrate the size of the fitting, the colour of the light emitted and reflected, the way in which it is distributed (which can be measured by instruments) and whether ugly shadows or patches of excessive brightness will occur. The sample will not, however, be viewed in the environment of the final installation, with the result that little realistic assessment can be made of the probability of glare nor any meaningful impression be gained by inexperienced people of the likely final appearance. Really effective trials are difficult to organize, and it may be better to view the effect of a proposal by visiting another church which has an installation similar to that proposed, bearing in mind that no two churches are alike.

External lighting

This includes floodlighting, access lighting and security lighting. The design considerations are different from those for interior lighting.

Floodlighting

As pointed out in Chapter 2, floodlighting benefits not only the church but also the community at large. However, economy in electrical consumption is important and it is not always necessary to illuminate the whole building: a selection of particular viewpoints and prominent features, provided that they do not appear to float improbably in space, can often produce a satisfactory result.

As with interior lighting the character and idiosyncrasies of the building should be assessed and emphasized by the lighting. Light striking a façade at right angles rarely reveals modelling and texture, and a long façade may need a range of fittings directed obliquely, all at similar angles, while deep shadows may need to be softened by suitable infill lighting. Clerestories set back from lower aisles can be lit from aisle roofs if care is taken to match the amount and direction of the light with that of the lower walls. The solidity of the building should always be revealed by ensuring that some light falls on return walls, even if those walls are not to be illuminated strongly. *See figure 13 as compared with figure 14.*

There are two light sources currently available which are suitable for floodlighting: high-pressure sodium and metal halide, the attributes of which have been described in Chapter 4. Care needs to be exercised if both sources are used for one building, but the colour contrast can be effective when used to emphasize a particular feature, for instance the internal illumination of a stone lantern, or to enhance the contrast between different building materials. Metal halide lamps are available which produce light in a variety of strong colours, but the effects possible are likely to be inappropriate for an ecclesiastical building, although they may sometimes be effective for lighting surrounding trees and vegetation.

There is a tendency to floodlight buildings too brightly. The guidelines published to guard against the escape of unwanted light into the sky or onto objects other than the one intended to be lit (light pollution) should always be followed (see the Bibliography in Appendix 6). Fittings should be chosen and sited so that the light falls on the building and does not also spill into the sky, so that passers-by or members of the congregation are not affected by glare, while gravestones or other unwanted features are not unintentionally highlighted. This can be achieved by using shields or louvres, but cutting out unwanted light produced from an unsuitably chosen fitting can be an expensive waste both in capital and running cost.

Fittings should be located to facilitate cleaning and lamp replacement. Those easily accessible to the public should be enclosed in a cage to prevent tampering or, in areas where vandalism is prevalent, mounted in a concrete or masonry bunker with metal grilles. However, little can be done to prevent determined theft.

Church lighting

fig. 13
A good example of external floodlighting, carefully displaying the various features of the building.

Photograph © NEP Lighting Consultancy

fig. 14
Floodlighting which fails to bring out the form of the buttresses and other features.

Lighting design: Bill Crawforth

Photograph © Mark Wood-Robinson

It is often useful, both to gain a high position for a fitting and also to remove it from the easy reach of vandals, to attach it to a tree. The tree must be sturdy and healthy enough for the purpose, and it will be necessary to trim the foliage from time to time. On no account should the trunk be encircled by a fixing band, and it is better to screw two or more stainless steel or galvanized metal bolts (*not* brass or copper) into pre-drilled holes, and attach a bracket on which the fitting can be mounted well clear of the trunk. Churchyard trees are often covered by tree preservation orders and specific approval from the local planning authority may be required regarding the method of fixing and the digging of trenches to the tree. In case of difficulty, expert arboricultural advice should be sought.

Towers and spires

Towers are particularly difficult to light so that the three-dimensional form is clearly expressed. It is more satisfactory to locate a fitting to illuminate two adjacent sides unevenly than one side by a beam at 90° to it and, if deep shadows are then thrown by buttresses, to soften them by secondary lighting. In order to obtain a good spread of light up the whole face of a tower a narrow beam grazing the faces from near the base, or two separate fittings to light the lower and upper halves from a more distant position, may be needed. While the former arrangement will exaggerate the texture of the masonry, the latter will tend to flatten it, and the effect can be unsatisfactory if the two different techniques are used on adjacent faces of the same building (*see figure 14*).

It is not unusual for the shadow of a roof to be projected across a tower, and a decision has to be made whether this will be acceptable or whether the layout of the lights should be altered to avoid it.

Spires are almost impossible to light evenly or without spill into the sky, and if there is access for maintenance they are best lit by fittings at the top of the tower which graze the surface. If the spire is conical three fittings will ensure that the whole surface is illuminated and also that the conical nature of the form is evident. In the case of octagonal spires adjacent faces should be illuminated to different intensities by adjusting the position of the fittings.

Stained glass windows

Stained glass windows can be lit from inside, but the effect is often disappointing compared with the appearance of the windows when the church is in use, and the interior appearance must also be considered.

Access routes

Access routes may be illuminated by reflected floodlighting, but most require independent sources which may be in the form of bollards, lanterns on posts or columns, or brackets or bulkheads mounted on the building. In locating these fittings care must be taken to ensure that the ground or steps are lit, and that pedestrians are not dazzled by the fittings; it is also desirable that people should be recognizable and not be seen merely as silhouettes.

Where there are trees and shrubs their appearance should be carefully considered when planning the lighting, and they should be made to look as attractive and natural as possible. It is better to err on the side of less rather than more light. Very little light indeed is needed to follow a path in the dark, but a pedestrian should be able to see beyond the lighted area to be satisfied that danger is not lurking in the darkness.

Security lighting

Security lighting may be provided by external lighting provided for other purposes, but it must be switched by a presence detector to give cover throughout the hours of darkness. The object is deterrence, and the very fact that a light comes on when approached is a deterrent. Suitable controls are described in Chapter 7, but the designer should ensure that all vulnerable points of the building are covered, and that the fittings cannot be disarmed easily.

The subject of this section is covered by the CIBSE guide LG06 *The Outdoor Environment* and by the CIBSE/ILE guide *Lighting of the Environment* with which lighting designers should be conversant. Only matters particularly relevant to churches have been mentioned above (see Appendix 6).

chapter 7
Controls

Switches

There must be means of switching all lighting on and off when required, and the switches or other controls should be placed where they are most convenient for the users, whether clergy, verger, organist, churchwardens, etc.

For simple installations it is important to find a convenient position where the main bank of switches can be mounted. This should preferably be where the lighting can be altered immediately before or possibly even during a service without disturbing the congregation. It could be in a western tower, or possibly in a vestry, depending on the relationship of the vestry door to the nave and chancel. It is desirable that the operator should be able to see as much as possible of the church from the switch position.

There must also be switches at the principal entrances and exits so that those entering and leaving can light their way to and from the main switches.

- For this purpose two-way switches are obviously most convenient.
- Where a few two-way switches are mounted on a larger panel the rest of which are one-way only, it is desirable to mark them in some special way.
- A convenient means of doing this is to form an indentation in the switch dolly with a drill and fill it with red varnish. A spot of varnish without such an indentation will soon wear off.

Switch panels with many ways can be confusing to operate.

- Where practicable the switches should be laid out as a miniature diagram of the church, for instance with the easternmost lights switched from the top row and the westernmost from the bottom.
- It is rarely possible to attain absolute clarity by such means, except in very small churches.
- The alternatives are to post a small chart beside the switch panel, or to have more than one switchplate. There might for instance be one plate for the nave, another for the aisles and a third for the chancel and sanctuary. All three plates should be clearly labelled to indicate which area they serve.

Switchplates are sometimes engraved to indicate the circuits controlled, but this is very inflexible and the engraving is liable to become out of date, if not positively misleading, within a few years. Labels or a small chart in a glazed frame are much easier to alter, and usually to read as well, especially if a small-scale diagram of the church is provided.

Chapels used only for special services are best switched locally with, of course, two-way switching for the routes to and from them.

It should not be forgotten that in many churches people will wish to practise on the organ when the building is otherwise empty, and switching for the route to the organ console is required.

In large churches it may be desirable to provide a 'master blackout' switch to ensure that all lighting is off when the last person leaves.

- It will then be necessary to ensure that all lighting is separately fed, to avoid turning off heating or other services at the same time.
- Where this facility is provided it may be more convenient to use one or more *contactors* – electrically operated switches which can be turned on and off by energizing or de-energizing a magnetic coil which takes very little current, and can operate at low voltage.
- It is likely to be cheaper to provide only light-duty wiring between the *contactor coils* and switches at the exit doors, rather than to divert the heavier duty wiring for all lighting circuits to the door positions.

Miniature circuit breakers

Miniature circuit breakers (mcbs) are increasingly used to protect electrical circuits instead of fuses. They are a sort of automatic switch which, in the event of a fault simply turn themselves off and, once the fault has been cleared, they can be turned on again by hand. It might save money to site a *distribution board* employing mcbs in some accessible position so that it can double the functions of circuit protection and switch panel.

However, mcb distribution boards are not things of beauty and are best placed either where they are not noticeable or concealed in a cupboard. The mcbs will be laid out in one or possibly two rows and any attempt at mimicking the layout of the lighting is impossible. Further, and perhaps more important, mcbs can only substitute for one-way switches. Where two-way switching is required for any circuits, two separate switches must be provided for each such circuit.

Whole and part switching

It is generally desirable to subdivide the circuits to give options such as the following:

- The church to be lighted at reduced power, either for casual visitors or for private prayer, or simply for use on dull days where a little extra lighting is required, but not very much; for instance, if there are three lights directed at the altar they might be switched as two and one, giving a choice of three separate levels of illumination.
- The nave and aisles should be switched separately.
- It may be better to divide each into west and east sections, for services when only a small number attend.
- Special functions like baptisms should also be allowed for.
- In some churches the choir may require lighting for longer hours during the week than any other users: arrangements for switching should take account of such factors.

Dimmers – types and application

A dimmer is a device which reduces the voltage in a lighting circuit, and so reduces the light output of lamps in that circuit which are suitable for dimming (see Chapter 4).

- Before the development of modern electronics dimmers were expensive, bulky and either gave out a great deal of heat or tended to hum.
- They were used for theatre lighting since there was no alternative but were impractical for use in a church, or in dwellings.
- Electronic dimmers still hum to a small extent, but reduce the amount of electricity used instead of wasting it as heat, although the efficacy (see Appendix 1) of the lamps reduces as the voltage is reduced.
- Reducing the voltage in a lighting circuit both reduces the light output and increases the life of incandescent lamps but may not necessarily increase the life of other types of lamp. Dimmers should not be installed purely as a matter of routine but only if increased lamp life or subtle control is actually needed.

Dimmers for voltage control only

As explained in Chapter 4, the mains voltage, in country churches especially, may be high during services. Electricity boards have in the past been allowed to vary the voltage by 6% up or down from its nominal value, but this is to be increased to a variation of 10%. However, a 6% increase in voltage will reduce the life of incandescent lamps by a third – that is from 1,000 hours to 660 hours approximately.

For many buildings the hours during which the voltage is high are likely to be roughly equal to those when it is low so that if the lamps are in use for long hours the overall effect on lamp life may not be important. However, this pattern may not hold for a church, in which case incandescent lamps may fail prematurely.

Voltage variation will also affect discharge sources, but not nearly to the same extent, except in those rare cases where the voltage falls so low that discharge lamps either fail to start, or flicker and go out for a time, perhaps as the organ blower motor starts up. However, if anything of that kind occurs there must be some very serious defect in the electricity supply, or possibly in the installation, and a full inspection should be made.

If there is reason to believe that the voltage is excessively high or low the Supply Authority should be asked to check it, if necessary by fitting a recording voltmeter for a week or two to study how the voltage does vary. Even if it is found that the voltage is often high there may be little the Authority can do about it unless it exceeds the permitted limits.

One solution is to fit one or more dimmers to the lighting system to drop the voltage to its proper value, or possibly even below it. For instance, lowering the voltage by 10% more than doubles the life of incandescent lamps, but decreases light output by about 30%.

Referring back to the discussion of the economics of light sources in Chapter 4, where access to lamps at high level is expensive, the best option may well be to fit dimmers to increase the life of incandescent lamps to, say, four years' usage. To maintain the same light output some additional lamps may be necessary, or their wattage may need to be increased. Overall, the *efficacy* – the amount of light obtained in relation to the amount of electricity consumed – will be reduced, and it will be necessary to check that the additional electricity consumption will not vitiate the advantage of longer lamp life. Each case has to be treated on its merits.

If dimmers are fitted purely for voltage control two policies are possible. The first is to fit the minimum number of large dimmers, and either to have them set to, say, a constant 90% of applied voltage, or, as a more sophisticated variation, to fit automatic control to hold the voltage constant at some value less than the nominal supply voltage. It is unlikely that the extra cost of the latter option will be justified in a church.

Dimmers for lighting control *(see also Appendix 5)*

Switches are the cheapest form of lighting control, but their effect can be uncomfortably abrupt while quite often some level intermediate between 'full up' and 'off' is required. Dimmers are increasingly used either to refine particular lighting settings, or to introduce some dynamic into the lighting. Unless all dimmers are maintained at full all the time (when there is no point in having them) an increase in the life of incandescent lamps, as explained on page 57, will then follow automatically.

Lighting which varies with time in this way is sometimes thought of as 'theatrical' or 'unnatural', but in fact gas lighting could always be dimmed while flame sources and daylight are always changing. This is apparently exploited in some, especially baroque, churches and it is fair to say that it is unchanging electric light which is really 'unnatural'. It is also worth noting that a book published in 1884 recommended turning the main gas tap down to reduce the glare of gas lights during the sermon.

Dimmers make it possible to alter the balance of light smoothly and without the slight shock inseparable from switching lights on and off, both to alter the focus of interest during the course of a service, or at the beginning or end of a concert or other special function.

The use of dimmers does not, of course, make it unnecessary to perform calculations at the design stage in order to ensure that sufficient light is available wherever it may be wanted. Indeed, it is likely that the use of dimmers will increase the amount of calculation required as it will be necessary to check that the division of the installation into separately dimmed circuits will be effective even when several of the dimmers may be set to give substantially reduced light.

Where it is intended to use dimmers to vary the lighting during services it is essential to use a system with which unskilled operators can produce acceptable results. Such automatic systems are discussed and explained more fully below.

Types of dimmer

There are basically three types of electronic dimmer: self-contained; remote, individually controlled; and remote, preset. Each type has characteristics making it particularly suitable for particular uses. All produce some noise, a buzz or hum.

Self-contained dimmers with rotary control knobs are commonly used in domestic situations, and can be used in churches for loads up to about

500 watts. They may be suitable for controlling one or two spotlights for the lectern or pulpit, but not for larger loads such as the chancel or part of the nave (see page 60).

Remote, individually controlled dimmers are separate units, generally sited near the main switchboard, and controlled by knobs, push buttons or sliders mounted at one or more remote positions. These dimmers are not limited as to load and 2 kW is a common size, while dimmers can also be linked so there is no restriction on what can be controlled in practice.

Several such dimmers are often mounted together in a common cabinet, which may also include fuses or circuit breakers so greatly easing installation. However, the noise generated makes it essential that they be mounted in a space that is separated from the congregation.

It is virtually impossible to operate four or five dimmer knobs together in an ordered way, so that with controls of this type any attempts to adjust the lighting during the service are bound to appear clumsy; similar, although less severe, difficulties apply to sliders. With push button control, changes in settings take place over periods of several seconds, so there is no need to operate all buttons simultaneously. For this reason, push button control is normally used for installations of moderate size.

Individual push button control plates are about the same size as multi-gang switchplates and typically there will be four illuminated buttons for each circuit or group of lights controlled. These might correspond to, say, maximum voltage (which need not necessarily be full mains voltage, see above), three-quarters light, half-light and out.

The time of fade can generally be adjusted when commissioning the system; about 20 seconds from full up to out is normally suitable.

In a small church each set of push buttons might be arranged to control groups of lights roughly as follows: chancel, choir, nave (east and west), north aisle, south aisle, chapels, etc.

Where there are more than about eight groups of lights to be controlled this arrangement becomes unmanageable even for an enthusiastic operator, and a preset control system is preferable.

Preset systems were originally developed for theatre lighting but are now commonly used in hotels where banqueting suites may include several rooms which are at times used individually and at other times combined into one. It is necessary to explain the normal usage of these systems, since the manufacturers do not always understand the special needs of churches and may assume that they require the same facilities as hotels. Push button plates are used, but in this case each button selects not just the individual setting of an individual circuit, but a complete arrangement of lighting.

In a church Preset 1 might be for choir practice, Preset 2 for Evensong, Preset 3 for Sunday morning services in winter, Preset 4 for Sunday services in summer, etc. Twenty settings will normally be enough and, depending on the details of the system selected, there might be 20 or more buttons.

Preset systems include an electronic memory which is normally programmed by the manufacturer, to the instructions of the lighting designer, when the system is first commissioned. It is essential to be able to alter this programme at any time when required and the best arrangement is to have a special programming unit which can be plugged into one of the fixed control plates when needed.

Control panels for remote control systems are generally connected as a 'daisy chain' using light-duty cable. They should be located at key points, including:

- exits, where full blackout should be one of the commands available;
- a main panel, possibly at a churchwarden's stall from which as much as possible of the church can be seen, and which should control all the lighting;
- any part of the church which is used independently.

With preset systems it is often useful to mount a small chart describing the function of each numbered setting beside each panel.

It is not necessary for all panels to be capable of controlling all circuits or presets, and the simplicity of the control wiring as compared with elaborate two-way switching can to some extent offset the cost of the dimming equipment.

The operator for any remote control system will require a 'cue sheet', indicating when changes take place and which buttons to press at each change. No special skill is needed.

Dimming for the pulpit and lectern

Even where the main lighting has an automatic control system, rotary knob domestic-type dimmers for spotlights on the pulpit or lectern may well be sufficient. The operations required for these spotlights are so simple that the cost of an extra automatic dimmer may not be justified.

Movement (presence) and photoelectric detectors

In churches which are left open for visitors but unattended, it may be worth considering the installation of a device which responds to movement, called a PIR (standing for *passive infra-red*) detector to bring on some lighting as people enter the building. These devices are often called presence detectors. There is rarely any difficulty in doing this, whether or not dimmers are in use. This avoids the necessity for the switches or controls to be accessible to strangers, who may in any case fail to switch off as they leave. If they are arranged to light the way to the main switch or dimmer control panel automatically, such detectors may make it unnecessary to have manual switches at the entrances.

The PIR detector, which is generally quite small, roughly a 75 mm (3 in) cube, must be mounted overhead within a few metres of the entrance door. Most such detectors have an adjustable minimum 'on' period, after which they will switch off unless they detect further movement.

Depending on the size of the church, it may be desirable to have more than one PIR detector so that the lights can be set individually or collectively to come on or remain on in each area as the visitor moves round the building.

Where lighting for visitors is only required during dull days or in the evening PIR detectors should operate with a photoelectric (PE) sensor, which holds the electric lighting off when the daylight is bright enough. Combined units are readily available (often used for porch lighting) but care is necessary to ensure that they are not influenced by the lighting they themselves control.

There must be means of disabling the PIR detectors during services, otherwise lights may come on and off when not wanted as people move about the building.

Interference with audio systems

There must be no interference with the public address, induction loop, or an electronic organ, from the dimmers. The dimming equipment itself should comply with British Standards and special care may be necessary with the routing and screening of wiring. More details are given in Appendix 5.

Control of external lighting

External lighting used purely for access might be controlled by a PE cell working in conjunction with a PIR (see above) with a timing device, which in darkness comes on and remains on for a minimum period of, say, ten minutes after detecting movement. There should also be a master 'on' switch inside the church to hold the lighting on continuously. Anyone coming to open up the church can then see their way in, and can switch the lighting on for all those who arrive later.

If the PIR detector is carefully sited it will also light the last person out, who will have turned off the master switch. Such detectors are normally sited above and near doorways. The PE cell must, of course, be screened from the lights it controls.

Lighting provided for security may be controlled as for access lighting, but there may be a need for additional security lighting, often tungsten-halogen floodlights, to protect parts of the exterior which are vulnerable to break-in, but have no external doors in frequent use, and have therefore no need of access lighting as such. Floodlights with PE/PIR cells built-in are readily available, and may be connected independently of the access lighting.

Floodlighting must obviously be controlled by time switch and unless it is intended to use it every night, there should be provision for omitting operation on certain days. The time switch should also have back-up in case of power failure. The older clockwork time switches have 'spring reserve' but the more modern electronic switches have battery reserve, often for a week or more. Setting the time switch to turn off at 11 p.m. or midnight is no problem, but there are various options for turning on.

Solar dial time switches are available which can be set to turn on at any time between one hour before and one hour after sunset daily, and are often used for street lighting. However, they are expensive and make no allowance for weather conditions and it is generally better to control switch-on by a light sensitive (PE) cell, connected in series with an ordinary time switch with day omission (i.e. provision to omit operation on any selected days of the week). Both devices then have to be on before the lights will work. If the time switch is set to come on at about 3 p.m. on the days required this will cover the darkest winter afternoon, but the PE cell will delay the actual time of switch-on until it is dark.

In addition to the automatic controls for the floodlighting there should be master 'on' and 'off' switches, the first for checking that the lamps are working without waiting for nightfall and for special occasions, and the second to make the system safe for servicing. To avoid abuse these switches should either be key operated, or labelled and sited in a locked room or cupboard.

chapter 8
Maintenance

Regular maintenance of lighting installations is essential, and suitable provisions should be included in any design.

The output of lamps, particularly discharge lamps, falls off as they age, while the reflectors and glasses of fittings become dirty. It is therefore most important that lighting equipment should be cleaned regularly and that consideration be given to changing lamps when their output has fallen substantially, even if they have not actually failed.

Access for cleaning and lamp changing is crucial to design, and may be particularly difficult in tall buildings, including many churches. There are two alternative approaches to the problem:

- The first is to ensure that all lighting equipment is easy of access, but this may limit the design in undesirable ways.
- The second is to ensure that access, although possibly difficult, is only required at relatively long intervals.

In practice both alternatives are usually employed: easy access for equipment in vestries, on choir stalls, etc. and sources with longer life at high level (see below).

Cleaning external reflectors at the top of a ladder can be very difficult, and of course, water should not be used. Several proprietary cleaning aids are available and in case of doubt the manufacturer should be asked to recommend a suitable type.

Reflector lamps do not normally need cleaning between replacement, hence their popularity where access is difficult. However, if they are run at such low voltage that their life is very long the front glass is likely to need cleaning every four years or so.

Group lamp replacement

In practice it is generally better to adopt what is called *group lamp replacement* for sources at high level. This means that all lamps at high level are replaced at specified intervals, which should be within their expected life. This will involve discarding lamps which are still working, but their residual value is likely to be trivial in relation to the cost of access. The work is generally carried out by an electrical contractor unless there is suitable and willing labour in the parish.

Lamps removed from high level which still appear to be in good condition can be specially marked, and reused in those fittings which are easy of access, but this may be more trouble than it is worth.

As explained in Chapter 4, one of the advantages of discharge sources is that they have long lives and access to them need be at longer intervals than for incandescent sources.

- However, as discussed in Chapter 7, the lives of incandescent lamps can be greatly increased by the use of dimmers so that the choice of lamp need no longer be dictated primarily by ease of access to it.
- It should be noted that a filament lamp stops working without warning when the filament breaks, whereas most discharge lamps show that they are nearing the end of the useful lives by becoming more difficult to start, or by flickering. The latter may, of course, be more disruptive than a lamp which stops working altogether.

To avoid these problems, it is desirable to design incandescent schemes with some *redundancy* – that is to ensure overlap between sources in order that the failure of one only will not be disastrous.

With discharge lamps an 'hours run' meter may be helpful to indicate when they are nearing the end of their rated life and trouble may be expected. It is not very difficult to arrange to illuminate a warning light in some suitable position when replacement is due.

Lamp identification

It is essential that the fittings are not disturbed during relamping, and that the correct size and type of lamp be used. Special care is necessary with reflector lamps which can be either of the 'spot' or of the 'flood' type, both identical in physical appearance.

The correct lamps should be marked on the record drawings, and possibly also by a small label or coloured indicator adjacent to the equipment itself, where it is invisible from the body of the church.

It is also desirable to mark the new lamps in some obvious way, to avoid an electrician having to peer at the lamp in bad light on top of a ladder to check that it is of the right type.

Aiming spotlights

Disturbance of the direction of spotlights during relamping is hard to avoid. Even if fittings have been tightened so far as possible when originally set up, they tend to work loose as a result of the constant heating and cooling during use. It is better to tighten up the locking very carefully before removing the old lamp.

The direction in which each lamp is pointing should be recorded. This might be by noting the position of the beam centre on a floor plan. Great care is necessary to ensure that the records are clear and accurate.

If the direction of spotlights has not been recorded at the time of installation it may be difficult to identify the precise direction in which they should be pointing unless each can be individually switched.

- Where spotlights cannot be switched individually somebody standing at ground level can locate the beam centre of each one by looking directly into the lamp and moving about until the glaring patch appears completely symmetrical.
- In many cases the shape of the filament can be seen in this position.

Maintenance

- If necessary, dark glasses should be worn during the operation, and/or the lamps kept dimmed.
- Having located the centre of each beam, this should be marked on the drawings.

Where it is impossible to clean or maintain a spotlight without disturbance it is desirable first to locate the beam centre and then mark the position on the floor. After adjustment the spotlight can then be directed back to the same position in accordance with instructions from someone standing at the required location for the beam centre.

Access equipment

Where seating is movable any of the normal range of access equipment, such as wheeled towers, may be used for high-level access. These have the advantage of being usable for building repairs and decoration as well as for lamp replacement. Sophisticated equipment operated hydraulically can be obtained on hire and the cost of purchase may occasionally be justified if it can be used for other types of maintenance work. However, nothing of this kind is feasible where there are fixed pews.

Fixed pews may even make the use of simple ladders very difficult and it may be worth making up a special board, padded on the underside and designed to rest across the tops of several pews, to support a ladder. The board should be fitted with fixed stops for the foot of the ladder and be designed so that several strong people can use it when hoisting the ladder into position.

Where a new installation is planned it may be advantageous to purchase the access equipment in advance and to inform the contractors that they may use it during the installation. This should save money by avoiding or reducing the need for special scaffolding, or for the contractor to hire equipment.

Where special equipment is purchased it is important to ensure that there is some suitable place to store it, and that it can be taken into and out of the building.

The value of access equipment can be greatly increased by providing the proper accessories. For instance, extension ladders should have pulleys and hoisting ropes so that they can be extended by someone standing at ground level. Detachable or lockable wheels may sometimes, but not always, be an advantage but one of the many forms of bracket to carry trays or containers at the top of the ladder is essential. It is sometimes forgotten that electricians, however skilled and strong, have only two hands each.

Pendants and chandeliers are sometimes installed on winches so that they can be lowered for relamping, but this is practicable only where there is an accessible roof void where the loose flexible cable can be coiled up as the chandelier is raised. Where there is no such void the winches have to be mounted on the side walls and the pendants connected by special automatic ('self-centring') plugs on the suspension plate of the chandelier which fit into sockets set in the ceiling. If these plugs ever jam it is necessary to erect scaffolding to free them.

Generally speaking, it is likely to be better and cheaper to provide stepladders or extending trestles for access to chandeliers and other equipment at moderate heights.

Extension ladders may be necessary for access to equipment at clerestory level but an aluminium ladder that will extend to 20 metres requires at least three strong people to manipulate it. This makes it scarcely practicable to replace lamps at high level individually as they fail, except where there is a substantial volunteer force of muscular people to assist. Group lamp replacement is likely to be the best option.

chapter 9
Conservation and safety

This chapter deals with two topics: the precautions necessary to minimize damage to delicate objects by lighting, and safety and escape lighting.

Lighting for conservation

All light damages fugitive materials, and not merely ultraviolet or sunlight. However, the damage is proportional both to the intensity of illumination (or, more correctly, *irradiance*, since non-visible radiation does damage) and to its duration. Other things being equal, short wave radiation (blue and ultraviolet) may do more damage than longer wave radiation (red and infra-red), but this is a complex subject.

Fluorescent tubes and certain other discharge sources emit some ultraviolet (UV) radiation but this can be screened out by the use of filters. Plastic jackets are available which slip over fluorescent tubes and screen out the UV: they can be reused when lamps are changed.

Incandescent lamps emit very little UV, but much more heat. Heat can cause damage both directly in inducing chemical change, and indirectly by drying, which may be disastrous for materials whose moisture content is important. Low voltage lamps are now available with *dichroic* reflectors. These reflect visible light but allow infra-red to pass through to the rear: the infra-red radiation is not then all directed at the illuminated object, but a large proportion can be dissipated to the air behind, provided that the fitting chosen has suitable arrangements for ventilation.

Another method of preventing either heat or UV reaching delicate objects is by using fibre optics. The technique is described in Chapter 5, and although expensive, it is often the most effective so the cost may well be justified where valuable and delicate objects are concerned.

Even when all precautions have been taken it is still better to minimize the hours of illumination of sensitive materials when they are not specifically required to be visible. For instance, a delicate altar cloth should not normally be exposed for daytime services if it is likely that sunlight will fall on it, but might be used for services on dull days and in the evenings if carefully and not too brightly lit, and covered immediately the service is over.

Valuable paintings or other objects in the church may be covered by curtains, drawn aside only for interested visitors. Another possibility is to place objects in situations screened from the general lighting in the building. Lighting in or on the display can be brought on for limited periods of, say, five minutes, by pushing a button. This enables interested visitors to view the object or painting without risk of serious damage.

For most fugitive materials there are recommended maximum illuminances called 'Thompson levels' which should not be exceeded in normal circumstances. Brighter lighting may be needed for photography, but should be used for the minimum period, and preferably only during exposure. For further information on lighting for conservation see the CIBSE guide *Lighting for Museums and Art Galleries* (see Appendix 6).

Lighting for safety and escape

Churches are not at the time of writing required to have safety lighting in accordance with BS 5266 as a matter of course. Nevertheless, lighting of this kind, generally called 'emergency lighting' may be necessary in crypts, especially those used as clubs, coffee bars, etc. while it is also desirable on tower staircases if the public is admitted.

Where churches are used for concerts, dramatic performances and similar functions the provision of emergency lighting will be a matter for discussion with the local authority. Whatever the financial constraints, the serious consequences to the church in the event of an accident, however trivial, should always be borne in mind.

The basic requirement for all emergency lighting is that both hazards and escape routes shall be marked and illuminated by two *independent* sources of electrical supply, which in practice means by both normal mains and by battery. In safety fittings and illuminated signs complying with BS 4533 the battery is normally built in and continually charged by the mains.

In many cases internally illuminated signs casting some downward light at the exit doors are all that is necessary, but where these doors lead not directly to the exterior, but to lobbies or staircases, it is important that there should be an illuminated sign or fitting at every set of doors, and at intermediate positions or landings, sufficient to ensure that the occupants can see their way to the exterior safely even in the event of a total mains failure.

Where the requirement is infrequent, painted signs illuminated by lanterns or torches with dry batteries may be sufficient, but in those churches used regularly for evening performances a proper system is desirable. The fittings can be demountable, on hooks, and plugged in as required, but the batteries should be kept on charge, as explained below.

Although the word 'EXIT' used to be regarded as sufficient for signs, the movement towards international standardization has led to the adoption of new British Standard signs with pictograms which some people consider inappropriate for use in churches. In such cases the authorities should be encouraged to accept either 'Exit', or 'Way Out' in a church in place of the 'running man' pictogram, although many are reluctant to deviate from recognized standards.

There are basically two types of illuminated safety sign, 'maintained' and 'non-maintained'. The first has (at least) two lamps, illuminated respectively by mains and a battery whenever the building is open. The non-maintained type has a battery lamp only and comes on only when the mains fail. The maintained type should be used where there is little or no daylight and when the normal lighting may be turned off, as may be the case for an evening concert or performance in a church.

It is not essential that the mains voltage and battery fed lamps be housed in the same fitting, and they can be separated so long as the switching is arranged appropriately.

In some cases it may be possible to convert existing fittings to safety use by using a 'conversion kit' including a rechargeable battery and extra lamp. However, most such kits are intended for linear fluorescent fittings, as are used in offices, and may be difficult to apply in churches, although they can be useful in places such as vestries, offices and crypts.

In crypts used for social occasions, clubs, meetings and similar activities, safety and escape lighting is highly desirable, as explained above. The maintained type is to be preferred, even if the local authority does not insist on it, since with this type of lighting the lamps and equipment are continually being tested.

The life of the rechargeable batteries used in safety and escape fittings is rarely more than five years and often as little as three. Most are designed to be kept on charge continuously, so even if fittings are taken down when not required, as suggested above, they should be left connected to a socket in a plant or store room, where the power is not turned off at night.

It is essential to follow the manufacturers' instructions carefully over the care and maintenance of rechargeable batteries. Instructions are packed with every fitting, and the more important ones are often printed inside the fitting as well.

The performance of the emergency fittings should be tested regularly, as described in *Wiring of Churches*.

Exit signs containing radioactive material which are self-luminous and require no power supply are available and are apparently attractive as they require no wiring. However, since April 2000 all such signs have had to be registered annually, for which there is a fee. This makes these signs no longer economical and they are better replaced by conventional types.

(See BS 5266 for further information on the requirements for emergency and escape lighting.)

appendix 1
The measurement of light – photometry

Early history

The astronomer Ptolemy of Alexandria in the second century AD, who classified stars by their brightness, was the founder of photometry. Stars barely visible to the naked eye were of the sixth magnitude, and the brightest of the first magnitude. The system is still in use today, although stars detected only by telescopes may have magnitudes up to 23 or more. In the nineteenth century the classification was standardized so that a star of given magnitude has a physical brightness 2.512 (the fifth root of 100) times greater than one of the next higher magnitude. This results from a fundamental aspect of perception: stars of magnitude from 1 to 6 appear to the eye to form a series of *equal steps* in brightness, but as measured by instruments they correspond to substantial *ratios* of energy.

It is only for simple stimuli like stars or patches of light that we can attach meaning to terms like 'equal steps of brightness' since in an ordinary scene we see not brightnesses but objects which are of different colours and appear to be more, or less, strongly illuminated. It must be emphasized that physical measurements bear no simple relationship to our perceptions of real objects.

Photometric units – candlepower

The first scientific measurements of terrestrial light were made in the eighteenth century and, as with stars, the fundamental concept is the power of a light source, that is to say, does it give a large amount of light or not?

- The standard first adopted was a particular grade of candle burning at a specified rate, giving about the same amount of light as a modern domestic paraffin wax candle.
- Total intensity is therefore often described as the candlepower of a source.
- Nowadays the standard is defined in a more sophisticated way, and is called the *candela* (cd), but is still approximately equal to that of an ordinary domestic candle.
- A source of candlepower 10 candelas emits 10 times as much light in total as a single candle, and so on.
- However, the emission of light generally varies with direction since some sources, like spotlights, emit light over a very limited range of angles while not even GLS lamps (or candles) can emit light through the base.
- The term *luminous intensity* (in candelas) is therefore used to describe the power of a source in a *given direction*.
- However, we often use the idea of a *uniform source*, whose intensity is the same in all directions, as a theoretical concept.
- We also use the concept of a *point source* for purposes of calculation, although all real sources must be of finite size.

- At distances of more than five times the largest dimension of a real source measurements obey the laws derived for theoretical point sources with sufficient accuracy for normal purposes.

Flow of light – luminous flux

We think of light flowing away from a source and the more powerful the source the greater the flow.

- The unit of *luminous flux*, as it is called, is the *lumen*, defined as the amount of light emitted *per unit solid angle by a uniform source of one candela*.
- For ordinary angles in a single plane a complete revolution is normally described as 360° but can also be described as 2π radians where one radian is the angle subtended at the centre of a circle by an arc equal to its radius.
- One radian is in fact 57.3°.
- An angle in three dimensions, called a *solid angle* and measured in *steradians*, is the *area* swept out on the surface of a sphere divided by the *square* of its radius (see figure 15).
- The total area of the surface of a sphere of radius r is $4\pi r^2$ and this, divided by the square of the radius (r^2) is simply 4π. There are therefore 4π *steradians* in a complete sphere. **It follows that a uniform source of intensity one candela emits 4π (12.57) lumens in total.**

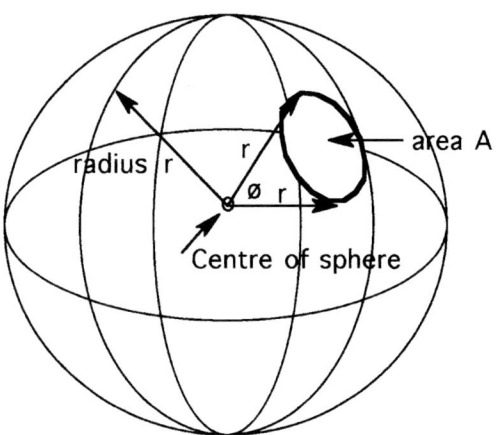

fig. 15
The concept of solid angle.

© Bill Crawforth

Solid angle ø = A/r^2 steradians

Illumination and illuminance

We are normally chiefly interested in the amount of light falling on a surface called, in common usage, the *illumination*.

- In lighting technology this word is now reserved for the process of lighting.
- For measurement of the amount of light falling on unit area of a surface the term *illuminance* is used.
- In SI (internationally agreed) units illuminance is measured in lux, and one lux is one *lumen per square metre*.

Appendix 1

- The imperial unit, the lumen per square foot, or *footcandle* is no longer used in the UK, but appears in older texts, and is still in use in the USA.
- The relationship is 1 footcandle = 10.76 lux (1m² =10.76 ft²).

We have seen that by definition a source of one candela emits 4π lumens, and a sphere of radius 1 m with such a source at its centre therefore receives 4π lumens over an area of $4\pi m^2$. Its average illuminance is therefore one lumen per square metre, or one lux. In other words:

One lux is the illuminance received from a candle at a distance of one metre.

Most recommendations for lighting are given as an illuminance measured on a particular plane, usually the horizontal for working environments, but increasingly often on the vertical. As explained in Chapter 2, in a church virtually the only important horizontal surfaces to be lit are the books of the congregation, while most other significant surfaces are non-horizontal.

Recommended illuminances

The illuminances listed below are likely to be found generally suitable for night time use:

Position	Illuminance (lux)	Plane of measurement
Body of the church	100 – 200	On the seats
Pulpit	250 – 300	On the face of the preacher
Lectern (and pulpit desk)	150 – 300	On the desk
Choir	150 – 250	On the music (as held up)
Chancel walls	100 – 150	
Altar	200 – 300	On the vertical as seen by the congregation
Vestries	200 – 250	Table top
Church halls	200 – 300	Floor

For church halls the figure given is suitable for public meetings, but for dances etc. 200 lux will be found too bright. In many cases a dual installation will be needed with special lighting for a platform and possibly dimmers on the main lighting, or part of it.

For each range of values in the list the lower figure represents the minimum that should be measured in any position, while the higher is the most that is likely to be necessary: it should not be taken as an average. There is no objection to exceeding the higher figure in some places, so long as the installation appears reasonably even. However, if the whole nave is lighted to 200 lux or more it may be difficult to achieve a subdued effect when required. This is the kind of situation where dimmers can be very helpful (see Chapter 7).

As proposed in Chapter 2, in the nave and aisles people with poor sight should be encouraged to sit in the better lit areas, but if they have sat in the same place for many years they may be reluctant to change.

The output of lighting equipment falls off markedly as the lamps age and the equipment becomes dirty (see Chapter 8). The recommended figures refer to the average over the life of the lamps and between cleanings.

In order to achieve this average the initial illuminance with brand new lamps and clean equipment is likely to be 40–50% greater.

Where lamps with integral reflectors have been used (see Chapter 4) the variation will be less since dirt is excluded, and only the reduction in light from the filament and front glass occurs. With tungsten-halogen lamps the reduction in output from the filament as it ages will be relatively less than for many other kinds of source.

The significance of illuminance figures

At first sight it seems strange that when many people can read by the light of a single candle, the light of between 100 and 200 candles at a distance of one metre is recommended for the nave of a church. However, as explained above, photometric quantities bear little or no simple relationship to our perceptions. Bright moonlight gives an illuminance of about 0.2 lux, whereas June sunlight can reach 80,000–100,000 lux. Since we have some sense of sight at levels far below bright moonlight the range of illuminances over which we can see our way about is over a million to one. However, we cannot see over this range of illuminances simultaneously: on going from a darkened room into sunlight we are dazzled for a minute or more, while on coming in again we can see little until our eyes have adapted to the lower light level.

The process of adaptation is fundamental to vision (and to perception in general) and it is important to understand that if we are to see well the range of illuminances within the field of view must not be too great. Many of us can just about (and, unfortunately, sometimes have to) follow a service with an illuminance of a few lux on our book, but if we then look up at a brightly lit chancel we may be dazzled, especially if some light sources are in view, and have to wait a few moments before we can see to read again.

Although we can attach very little meaning to one sort of lighting looking so many times brighter than another, it is clear that although 200 lux is a lot brighter than 1 lux, it certainly does not look as if there were 200 candles just behind our heads, and again, although sunlight may be agreeable, it does not make us think of 100,000 candles at a distance of one metre. Illuminance recommendations are based on what has been found by experiment to satisfy most people in practice: they are difficult to interpret in perceptual terms.

Reflectance – luminance

We can see objects only because they reflect light to our eyes: white objects reflect all colours equally and to appear white in white light they have to reflect about 70% or more of the total light falling on them. If they reflect much less they may appear pale grey in a normal environment. The *reflectance* is a number less than one indicating the proportion of light reflected, and coloured objects appear coloured because they have different reflectances for different wavelengths in the spectrum. As stated, white

Appendix 1

objects have a (uniform) reflectance of 0.7 or 0.8, while dark objects may have a reflectance of only 0.02 or 0.03. It is surprisingly difficult to produce a surface which reflects no light at all.

Sometimes reflectance is expressed not as a number less than one, but as a percentage: it is then generally called the reflection factor. In the Munsell system of colour specification the term 'value' is used. Colours of high value have high reflectances, and of low value have low reflectances, but 'value' seeks to relate to our perception of 'lightness' rather than to the proportion of light reflected and the relationship between the two measures is complex.

As a general rule, the higher the reflectance the lighter the colour. A surface which reflects 55% of incident light in total, but more red than other colours, might appear pink. A surface which reflects the same proportion of colours throughout the spectrum but only 15% of incident light in total may appear as a dull red.

As explained above, in a natural environment the *illuminance* varies greatly from dawn until dusk, but the *reflectance* of objects surrounding us does not vary.

- Our visual system responds primarily to these reflectances, and to the sudden changes in reflectance at the outlines of objects.
- It is by these means that we are able to see objects in their true colours despite enormous variations in lighting.
- These phenomena are called variously *'lightness constancy'*, *'brightness constancy'* and *'colour constancy'*. The distinction between them is not always clear.

Light which is neither reflected from nor transmitted through a surface is absorbed, and appears as heat.

The light given out per unit area of a surface is called its *luminance*. The similarity of this word to 'illuminance' is most unfortunate and new terminology is badly needed. The SI unit of luminance is the *candela per square metre (cd/m^2)*.

Surfaces which give out light may be themselves luminous, like fluorescent tubes, or transparent or translucent so that light comes through them, like an opal glass lampshade. In either case their luminance is given by I/A, where I is the intensity in a given direction in candelas and A the projected area in the same direction.

The same term, luminance, is used to describe surfaces which merely reflect light: the relationship between the illuminance, reflectance and luminance of a matt opaque surface is:

$$\textit{luminance (cd/m}^2\textit{)} = \frac{\textit{illuminance} \times \textit{reflectance}}{\pi}$$

A *matt* surface is defined as one that reflects light equally in all directions and its luminance will therefore be the same when viewed from any direction. Glossy surfaces reflect preferentially away from the source and their luminance varies both with the direction of illumination and of view (see *figure 16*).

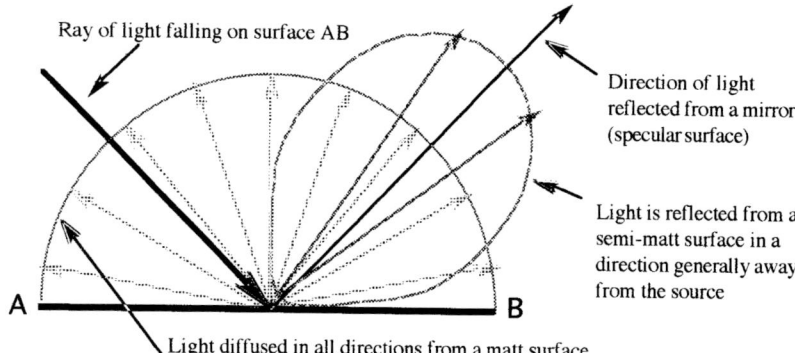

fig. 16
Diffuse, spread and specular reflection.

© Bill Crawforth

Most materials found in churches are effectively matt, with the exception of polished altar crosses or other special ornaments. These can create acute problems with lighting because they can be distractingly bright in directions which reflect the sources, and almost dark seen from other directions.

The relatively small amount of sheen on marble or other polished stone tablets is rarely a serious problem, and yet should be borne in mind when arranging lighting for them, especially if they can reflect the image of a light source.

Contrast

Although contrast may be of many kinds – in shape, texture, colour, etc. – in lighting engineering it refers to contrast in luminance only. If an object of luminance L_1 is seen against a background of luminance L_2 the contrast between the two is said to be $(L_1 - L_2)/L_2$, that is to say, the difference between the two luminances divided by the background luminance.

If an object is brighter than its background the formula for contrast gives a positive number, but if the object is darker than the background the formula gives a negative number. This difference is often ignored (as if white ink on black paper were as easy to read as black ink on white paper, which is rarely true), but this is a highly complex matter.

In studies of 'visual performance' (the relationship between lighting and ease of seeing detail), contrast can be very important.

Simultaneous contrast describes the fact that juxtaposing two different colours (possibly, but not necessarily, with a white or black band between) heightens the visual impact of each. By such means striking effects can be obtained without any significant difference in luminance.

Brightness

We have described *luminous intensity*, the brightness of a source of light; *illuminance*, the brightness of lighting; *reflectance*, related to the brightness of a colour; and finally, *luminance*, the brightness of a surface. 'Brightness' can have so many meanings that it is best avoided altogether in serious discussions of lighting. The term 'apparent brightness' is used to describe the 'subjective response' to a visual stimulus. However, we do not normally see 'brightnesses', but objects of different colours which appear to be more, or less, strongly illuminated. In scientific research 'apparent brightness' can be defined by the method used to measure it in any particular investigation, but it is never clear what, if any, relationship this bears to other investigations, let alone to ordinary perception.

People have at times tried to devise methods of lighting design based on concepts such as 'apparent brightness', and while talented designers can often produce good results even when their theories are defective, the concept is of very limited utility. Since it takes little or no account of lightness and colour constancy it can in some cases be positively misleading and is best avoided altogether. Arguably, the only really successful application of 'apparent brightness' is in assessing the magnitudes of stars (page 70) but this is a far cry from lighting parish churches.

Luminous output – efficacy

The output of an individual light source is expressed in *lumens* but in comparing different kinds of source we wish to know how much light each type gives for a given electricity consumption. This is expressed as *lumens per watt* and is called the *efficacy* of the source. The word is derived from 'efficiency', but the latter might include all kinds of other measures apart from lumens per watt, such as ease of installation or its shape or colour being especially suitable for a given application, etc.

For sources which need external control gear it is important that figures quoted for efficacy allow for the electricity consumed by the control gear itself but sometimes manufacturers evade this issue by quoting what is called '*lamp efficacy*', that is, they ignore control gear losses. The excuse sometimes given is that control gear of different types may have different losses for the same lamp, but the differences are rarely significant.

Fluorescent tubes operating at high frequency are a special case since their efficacy is substantially greater than when operated at mains frequency, and is normally quoted as a figure separate from that for mains frequency use.

Such problems do not, of course, arise with lamps which do not need control gear at all, or where the gear is integral with the lamp.

appendix 2
Glare

Glare arises when some part of the visual field appears excessively bright. We can distinguish between discomfort glare, which causes discomfort or dissatisfaction without affecting our ability to see clearly, and disability glare in which our ability to see is impaired.

Disability glare should be rare in churches, but may occur when direct sunshine through a window prevents our seeing anything beside the window, or if unsuitable floodlights have been mounted above, say, the crossing, making it impossible to see the upper parts of the tower when looking upwards. Another common problem is where an excessively bright east window makes it difficult to see the altar clearly.

Discomfort glare has been extensively investigated for offices, classrooms and similar spaces and effective predictive techniques have been developed. However, these are chiefly applicable to regular arrays of lighting equipment mounted on or suspended below the ceiling of a rectangular room. In a church such techniques are difficult to apply, partly because the mathematics will be much more complicated, partly because there are also reasons for thinking that the bases of judgement for lighting in a church are different from those in a space intended primarily for working.

It is easy to list the parameters which are likely to affect the probability of glare using only common sense, as follows.

- The luminance of the light source(s)
- The number of light sources
- The size of the light sources
- The positions of the light sources in relation to the normal direction of view: sources in front of our eyes must cause glare more often than if we only see them when we look upwards.
- The contrast between the light source(s) and the background: it is a matter of common experience that a source seen against a light background is less glaring than when seen against a dark one.
- The ambient lighting conditions: a bare lamp in a dark room might appear glaring, but in a light room it might hardly be noticed. At night we are dazzled by car headlights but by day we can hardly see if the lights are on.

Although strict application of glare prediction methods is difficult in churches, some general comments are relevant. In particular, the luminance of a source is more important in causing glare than its size. If, therefore, we fit a lamp into a diffusing shade we increase the visible area and reduce the luminance of the light source in roughly the same ratio so that, overall, glare is reduced. This is the basis of most practical methods of glare control.

Unfortunately, the luminance of the source is also much more important in causing glare than are bright ambient conditions in reducing it. If we take opal glass shades which do not glare when fitted with 60 watt lamps and fit

Appendix 2

150 watt lamps instead (assuming that they will go in, and will not overheat) we will have increased both the luminance of the sources and that of the ambient lighting. However, the former is more important and, overall, glare will be increased. This is why it is so difficult to increase the illuminance from pendants with diffusing glass shades merely by increasing lamp sizes, without creating glare.

Beyond drawing attention to all such matters, it is hard to give general advice about glare control in churches. Some particular problems are discussed in Chapter 6, dealing with certain aspects of design. It is also worth stressing that the glare method published by CIBSE for use in rectangular rooms lit by a regular array of fittings cannot usefully be applied in any normal church.

For choirs, and musicians generally, there are always conflicts. Light on their faces may give rise to vociferous complaint of glare and light from behind or vertically overhead onto the music will be requested. Lighting from these directions will leave the faces largely in darkness, and/or looking most unpleasant (*see figures 2 and 8*): care and compromise are always necessary.

appendix 3
Colour

Colour of light

Although white generally seems to us simpler or 'purer' than other colours, in fact to a physicist light is *electromagnetic radiation* and each specific spectral colour has its characteristic *wavelength*. White light is a complex mixture of all spectral wavelengths which can be separated as in a rainbow or by a prism. We talk loosely of 'white' or 'red' light but, of course, the light rays themselves have no colour, but are so called because they stimulate our visual system to perceive colour.

When we heat a poker in the fire it glows first a dull red then a brighter red, then yellow until finally it becomes 'white hot'. Incandescent bodies give out radiation over a wide range of frequencies, but at temperatures of between about 1,000° and 8,000° much of this radiation is visible light, and as the temperature increases, the peak intensity shifts through the spectral range red – orange – yellow – green – blue – violet. In fact, we never see anything 'green hot' since there is always so much radiation of other types which swamp the green colour, and the appearance is 'white hot'. Notionally, at very high temperatures the peak shifts so far that the red and yellow output will start to fall off so that we can see objects which are 'blue hot'. Some distant stars are often described as blue, but nothing at that temperature is normally seen on earth, although a blue sky approximates to it in appearance for rather different reasons.

We can therefore characterize the range of colours all of which seem 'white' by what is called their colour temperature (CT). The *lower* the colour temperature the yellower or *'warmer'* the light, while the *higher* the CT the 'whiter' or *'colder'* the light. Although colour temperature is defined with reference to a theoretical incandescent 'black body' to which real objects can only approximate, for most practical purposes we can say that ordinary incandescent lamps have a CT of about 2,700°, sunlight about 4,800°, average daylight around 6,500° and light from the north sky 8,000° or more.

In comparing the effect on coloured objects of different kinds of 'white' light we might note that flame sources and, to a lesser extent, incandescent lamps make blues seem rather dull, whereas bright sunlight makes all colours more vivid. However, we are unlikely to complain that the colours are 'distorted' by any of these sources.

Colour temperature is measured in degrees Kelvin. These are similar to degrees Celsius, but 0° Kelvin is 'absolute zero' (–273°C). Degrees K = degrees C + 273. As most colour temperatures are measured in thousands of degrees, the difference in practice is rarely very significant.

When it comes to discharge lamps the position is more complicated. Since their light emission is not due primarily to heat, its composition does not necessarily correspond even approximately to that of an idealized 'black body' and our visual system finds much more difficulty in adjusting to it. The extreme case is the yellow sodium street lamp: the low pressure version of this lamp (SOX) gives out only yellow light, so that although it is apparently highly economical it gives no indication of colours at all.

For street lighting and heavy industry, where discharge lamps were used at first, accurate rendering of colours is not necessarily very important, but their application to shops, offices, homes and so on has depended on producing lamps which make colours look natural. Although there are now many kinds of discharge lamp which do display colours well, they are not always used appropriately.

As explained in Appendix 1, white surfaces reflect all visible wavelengths equally but coloured surfaces reflect some wavelengths more strongly than others. The light reaching our eyes from any object will therefore depend not merely on its reflectance in different parts of the spectrum but also on the composition of the incident light.

The effect of a light source on coloured objects is called its *colour rendering* and in the case of some discharge sources this can be disagreeable, especially on food and faces since we tend to interpret their colours as indications of palatability and health, respectively. In this respect discharge sources differ from flame and incandescent sources and from daylight, whose effect on coloured objects is rarely found disagreeable.

Specifying the colour effect of light sources

In describing the colour effect of any light source at least two parameters must be specified. The first is the *correlated colour temperature* (CCT) which specifies whether the source is 'warm' or 'cool' in appearance (see page 79). A source with a CCT of 2,700° will have much the same appearance as an ordinary electric light bulb, whereas one of CCT 4,500° will appear distinctly cool. The word 'correlated' has to be used since no real light source is exactly like a black body but the CCT means the temperature of the black body which the light output of the source most resembles.

The second measure of interest is the way in which the source renders colours, as explained above. The body responsible for international agreement on lighting is the *Commission Internationale d'Eclairage* (CIE). The CIE 'colour rendering index' (Ra) is the system universally used to characterize light sources.

The CIE system involves comparison between the effect of a particular source on a number of standard colours with that of a perfect 'black body radiator' of the same CCT, for which the index is set at 100. For interior lighting where good colour rendering is required sources with an index of 80 or more should be chosen.

However, the colour rendering index has the defect of all single figure indices, in that it is trying to compress a vast amount of data and cannot make subtle distinctions.

The CIE index seeks to give equal weight to many colours, which means that it cannot regard any one as being specially important. Two sources might each have a Ra of 85, which is quite good for normal interior lighting, but one may be more accurate with blues and the other with reds. The latter would obviously be preferable in an interior in which differing shades of red were especially important, and might even be better than another source with an index of, say, 88, if that source were not especially good with reds.

There is another problem called 'metamerism'. This means that two surfaces which appear to match under one kind of light source may not necessarily match under another. Its occurrence depends on subtle interactions between the distribution of wavelengths in the sources and the variation of reflectance with wavelength of the surfaces.

It is therefore always desirable to conduct trials wherever it is intended to change light sources in a given location. For the reasons explained above, these trials should preferably be on site using the actual materials and objects involved. Colour sample cards cannot be relied upon.

There are two other problems with the CIE colour rendering index:

- The first is that the CCT for some sources may be practically meaningless. For instance, a pinkish source does not resemble a hot body at any temperature and its notional CCT and the colour rendering index may be misleading.
- Second, people do not always prefer a source which resembles a black body and in certain cases 'distorted' colours are actually preferred.

As explained in Chapter 4, the colour appearance of a light source should always be distinguished from its colour rendering. Colour appearance refers only to the effect of the source when viewed directly, but in fact most light sources – even those with very poor colour rendering – look approximately 'white' under these conditions and it is not therefore possible to judge the colour rendering of a source merely by looking at the source itself.

It must once again be emphasized that colour phenomena are very highly complex and in case of doubt site trials are always to be recommended.

appendix 4
Contract clauses

It is recommended that the following clauses (or their equivalent) be included where appropriate in any specification for a new lighting installation in a church, especially where it will continue in use during the works. These clauses are in addition to the list at the end of Chapter 3, pointing out those matters, apart from the work itself, which should be covered in the contract, and supplementary to those on pages 10 and 11 of *Wiring of Churches*.

Avoidance of disruption
- The Contractor is working in an occupied building and the safety of the Purchaser's staff and visitors shall at all times be properly preserved by the Contractor. (*It may be desirable to add a note about the likely average age of the congregation.*) (In Building Contracts the person or organization for whom the work is being carried out is normally called 'The Employer'. For contracts where only electrical (or heating) work, and no building, is required, the same person or organization is called 'The Purchaser'. These words are purely matters of custom, and either may be used.)
- Where appropriate it must be stressed that the church will continue in use throughout the progress of the works and the Contractor's gear shall be cleared away to permit services and other activities to proceed unhindered and in safety.
- The Contractor will be required to make the necessary arrangements with the minister or an authorized representative at daily or weekly intervals, defining those areas where work is to be carried out and the Contractor shall, so far as is reasonably practicable, arrange the places of work to fit in with the normal operation of the church. In particular, areas required for use must be left clear and clean at the end of each working day.

Builders' work
- Except where expressly authorized by the Purchaser or representative, the Contractor may not carry out any work on the fabric of the building which may cause damage or defacement. Except where screwed traps already exist, the Contractor is not to lift floor boards nor cut away nor remove any timber or decorated plaster work, etc. without prior permission. All such work must be carried out only by skilled workers nominated or approved by the Purchaser, and the Contractor shall give reasonable notice of such requirements so that appropriate arrangements can be made.
- Where the Contractor must provide fixings to walls, etc. in finished areas, the position and nature of these fixings must be agreed in advance. The Purchaser or Engineer may direct that any such holes or fixings be provided by skilled workers nominated or approved by the Purchaser.
- The specialist contractor or skilled workers carrying out such builders' work may be sub-contracted to the Electrical Contractor, or directly

retained by the Purchaser, as may be decided by the Architect, Engineer or Project Manager.
- Without prejudice to the above, the Contractor should allow in the tender for all necessary routine builders' work, such as cutting away and making good in the intake cupboard, stores, ceiling voids and other areas where there are no special finishes which might be damaged. However, such work is in all cases subject to the consent of the Purchaser or representative.

Protection of contents, wall paintings, etc.
- Consultations with the Purchaser's representatives shall include the identification, well in advance, of those items in and around the building which will need protection. Adequate time must be allowed for specialist staff to remove or protect these items as appropriate before any work is started.
- The Contractor shall also allow for providing sufficient clean dust sheets to protect the building and such items as are not removed from working areas, from dirt and damage, and for protection of any delicate items which might be liable to damage.

Work in or near the organ
- Where work is required in or near the organ the Contractor shall approach whoever is responsible for maintaining the organ well in advance, obtain agreement to what is to be done, and comply with any necessary protective measures.

Aiming and training lighting fittings
- The aim and exact location of all fittings shall be discussed before installation and shall be confirmed by a site trial after dark with a sample fitting of each type on a temporary lead. Where possible the aim of each fitting shall be locked mechanically after this has been verified by trial.

Availability of light fittings
- The fittings specified are to be placed on order at the commencement of the Contract. Any problems with delivery or availability shall be reported immediately. Unauthorized substitution of lamps or equipment will not be permitted.

appendix 5
Precautions with dimming systems

Quite simple types of dimmer will suffice for mains voltage incandescent lamps, but where transformers or the control gear of linear fluorescent tubes, etc. are involved special precautions have to be taken. Except where the manufacturer specifically states that the dimmers are equally suitable for mains incandescent, low voltage and discharge sources, it is important to check that each dimmer is suitable for the type of source it will actually feed.

Dimmers suffer from the same problems as all other electronic equipment – too many individual designs, frequent component changes and insufficiently thorough testing of prototypes before going into production. They are also designed by electronics engineers who have a habit of assuming that they really understand lighting without having thought much about it, and the more sophisticated the control the more pronounced these problems can be.

One of the most common difficulties is the so-called *dimming characteristic*.

- Dimmers are scaled, or marked, typically either from 1 to 10 or sometimes from 1 to 100.
- We would naturally wish half of full-scale setting to be about 'half-light', but it is difficult to say what this actually means, and even if there were some reliable way of defining it, the precise voltages at which different fractions of full output appear vary from one type of source to another.
- As pointed out in Chapter 7, dropping the voltage of an ordinary incandescent lamp by about 10% reduces light output by 30%. If the scale of the dimmer is simply related to voltage, the light will drop by 30% from dimmer setting 10 to 9, and the lamp will be virtually out by setting 5 or 6.
- Few commercial dimmers are quite as bad as that, but in many products no light is visible until setting 3, and there is a very big jump between, say, 4 and 6.

Even those dimmers which have a reasonably good characteristic for incandescent lamps may be less smooth for tungsten-halogen and low voltage lamps, and possibly wildly out for fluorescent tubes. Again, it is important to check in advance with manufacturers, and the best designs should have some means of adjusting the dimmer characteristic after installation.

It is difficult to give specific advice as to which kind of dimmer, control or memory system is likely to be the best for the following reasons:

- Particular systems may be especially suitable for particular churches.
- Existing systems are being refined and new ones introduced all the time.
- This has the advantage that the facilities nominally available are constantly increasing.

- It also has the disadvantage that it usually takes several refinements to ensure that a system works fully reliably in all circumstances, so that whenever a major change is made in the circuit, this process of refinement has to start all over again.

Experience has shown that certain precautions are very desirable in specifying and installing dimmer systems.

- Confirm with the manufacturer that the system will operate correctly over the range of voltage variation permitted to the electricity supply authority. Factories tend to be in industrial estates with a good modern electricity supply and manufacturers are sometimes genuinely unaware that their dimmers may become unstable if the voltage goes down by 6 or 10%.
- Especially where low voltage transformers or control gear for fluorescent lamps are involved, confirm that there will be no 'buzzing' or 'humming' from the lamps or gear.
- Require specific acoustic performance data, such as NR 25 as background noise level, or 20 dBA measured at a distance of 1 m and do not accept statements such as 'the system will be totally silent'. Some electronics engineers are surprisingly ignorant of acoustics.
- Most dimmer cabinets will emit some noise, and should be mounted in a separate room where they will not be audible to the congregation.
- Some manufacturers of dimming systems ask for full payment in advance, including payment for commissioning, but this should in no circumstances be agreed.
- If the manufacturer is genuinely concerned about the financial stability of the contractor or purchaser the money can be held by a stakeholder.
- Very few complex dimming systems work absolutely correctly first time and the church should not be left helpless with an ineffective system while the contractor and manufacturer blame each other.
- It might be reasonable to pay 60% of the cost of the equipment on delivery to site and a further 20% when installed and functioning.
- The final payment, including the cost of commissioning and programming, should be made only when the system is working correctly.

It is hoped that in due course standards will be developed for dimming systems so that problems of the type described above will no longer appear. However, establishing standards in a field that is still developing rapidly always risks doing more harm than good.

Interference with audio systems

It is necessary to ensure that there is no interference with the public address or induction loop systems, or an electronic organ, from the dimmers. The dimming equipment itself should comply with British Standards in this respect, but special care may be necessary with the routing and screening of wiring.

In particular, mains voltage wiring, especially to dimmed circuits, should be kept at least 300 mm away from audio wiring, and more if the two run parallel for more than a metre or two. Metallic screening of one or both

Appendix 5

types of wiring is desirable, and they should never be run in the same trunking, even if this has separate compartments. If the two types of wiring have to cross each other they should do so at right angles, and if there is no space to maintain wide separation between them, an earthed metal sheet should be fixed between the two.

appendix 6
Bibliography

Books

Brown, R.J.	*The English Village Church*, Robert Hale, 1998
Gombrich, Ernst	*Art and Illusion*, Phaidon Press, 1962
Gregory, Richard Harris, John Heard, Priscilla Rose, David (eds)	*The Artful Eye*, Oxford University Press, 1995
O'Dea, William	*The Social History of Lighting*, Routledge & Kegan Paul, 1958

CIBSE Reports and Guidance Notes

LG06	*The Outdoor Environment*, CIBSE, 1992
LG08	*Lighting for Museums and Art Galleries*, CIBSE, 1994
ILE01	*Lighting of the Environment: A Guide to Good Urban Lighting*, CIBSE (published jointly with the Institution of Lighting Engineers), 1995

Booklets published by the Council for the Care of Churches

Bordass, William Bemrose, Colin	*Heating Your Church*, Church House Publishing, 1996
Sage, Andrew	*Wiring of Churches*, Church House Publishing, 1997

British Standards

BS 5266	*Emergency and Escape Lighting* (including latest amendments)
BS 7671	The IEE Regulations for Electrical Installations (including latest amendments – now a British Standard)

Background information

CIBSE Code

The recognized standard for lighting in this country is the Code for Interior Lighting published by the Chartered Institution of Building Services Engineers, Delta House, 222 Balham High Road, London SW12 9BS. Those who wish to go more deeply into the design of lighting should study the Code.

The recommendations of this guide are similar to, but not in all cases identical with, those in the Code.

Building Regulations

These are mandatory in new buildings or major refurbishments and are administered by the local authority. Part L is concerned with energy conservation and is currently under revision, but requires a major proportion of lighting to be provided by means other than tungsten sources, except where this would be impractical. The application of the revised edition to churches is not clear at the time of writing.

Construction Design and Management (CDM) Regulations

Administered by the Health and Safety Executive these regulations ensure that building work is carried out under safe working conditions. Except for minor works it is necessary to register proposals with the Executive and demonstrate that risk has been assessed and how it will be managed. All work must meet these conditions, but notification is not normally required for works taking less than 30 working days with not more than five workers on site (500 person hours). While contractors can reasonably be expected to ensure that they will not put their employees at risk, the risk to be incurred by an employee during maintenance subsequent to completion of an installation is a matter for the designer to consider.

English Heritage

English Heritage is based at 23 Savile Row, London W1S 2ET (tel: 020 7973 3000) where advice about the office covering the particular church can be obtained. The local office can advise whether any other historical body will be interested.

Index

access equipment for maintenance 65–6
access routes 53–4
advice, specialist 3, 14, 15, 16
altars 43–4
archaeologist, consultation with 15, 17
architect, inspecting 3, 15, 19
architectural considerations 4–5, 40–41
art, works of, and conservation 46–7, 67–8
audio systems, interference with 61, 85–6

balance of internal lighting 42
beam of light, measurement of direction of 50
bollards 35
brackets, exterior 35
brief, preparation of 14
brightness, use of term 75–6
builders' work 82–3
building regulations 88

candle lamps 22–3
candlepower (measurement) 70–71
ceiling-mounted fittings 34
CFL (compact fluorescent lamps) 26–7
chandeliers 30, 36–7, 65–6
checklist for project planning 13–14
choir stalls 44–5
circuit breakers 56
cleaning *see* maintenance
colour of light 20, 21–2, 79–81
compact fluorescent lamps (CFL) 26–7
concealed fittings 37–9
conservation, lighting for 46–7, 67–8
consultation process 3, 15
contractor, electrical 14, 15–16
  contract clauses 82–3
contrast in luminance 75
controls, lighting 55–62
costs of lighting 29–32

DAC (Diocesan Advisory Committee) 3, 14, 15, 17
daylight in relation to electric light 9–10
decorative fittings 36–7
design
  development of 15–16
  external lighting 51–4
  interior lighting 40–50
diffusers 33
dimmers 56–60
  precautions with 32, 84–6
Diocesan Advisory Committee (DAC) 3, 14, 15, 17
discharge lamps 14, 20–21, 25–9
  economics of 29–32
distribution board 56
downlighting 49
dramatic performances 48
dramatic use of lighting 10–11

economics of lighting 29–32
electricity
  costs 29–32
  introduction of 2–3
  in relation to daylight 9–10
  supply 13–14
  see also light sources
emergency lighting 68–9
emphasis, lighting for 6–8, 42, 43–8
English Heritage 15, 88
exit signs 68–9
exterior fittings 35–6
external lighting control 61–2
external lighting design 51–4
eye conditions and lighting 9, 42

faces, lighting of 6–8
fading control *see* dimmers
fibre optics 35, 67
filament lamps *see* incandescent lamps
fittings, lighting 33–9
floodlighting
  external 5, 35, 51–3, 61
  internal 34–5, 49
  and stained glass 9
floor standing fittings 34
fluorescent lamps, shaped 26–7
fluorescent light 20
fluorescent tubes 25–6
fugitive materials 67–8

gas lighting 2
glare 14, 43, 77–8

halogen lamps 23–4
hidden fittings 37–9

identification of lamps 64
illuminance
  for fugitive materials 67–8
  for reading 41–2
  recommended 72–3
  use of term 71–2
  visual performance 8–9
incandescent lamps 20, 22–5
  economics of 29–32
induction lamps 28–9
installation 17–19
insurer, church 15, 19
interior lighting
  design 40–50
  fittings 34–5

lamp standards 36
lamps
  identification 64
  replacement 31, 63–4
  types of 20–32
layout drawing 18
lecterns 45, 60
LEDs (light emitting diodes) 29
light
  colour of 20, 21–2, 79–81
  measurement of 70–76
  quantity of *see* illuminance
  sources 20–32
  as a symbol 1, 4
lighting
  for conservation 46–7, 67–8
  consultants 3, 14, 15, 16
  controls 55–62
  costs 29–32
  design 15–16
    external 51–4
    internal 40–50
  dramatic use of 10–11
  fittings 33–9
  floodlighting *see* floodlighting
  gas 2
  glare 14, 43, 77–8
  history of 1–3
  maintenance 51–3, 63–6
  modelling by 6–8, 43, 49
  project planning 13–19
  security 5, 36, 54, 61, 68–9
  specialists 3, 14, 15, 16
  techniques 48–50
linear lamps 23, 25–6
luminaires 33–9
luminous flux 71
luminous output, efficacy of 76

maintenance 51–3, 63–6
measurement of light 70–76
metal halide lamps 28

89

Index

modelling by lighting 6–8, 43, 49
modern churches 11–12
monuments and conservation 46–7, 67–8
movement detectors 60–61
musical performances 48

neon lamps 25–6

paths 53–4
pendant fittings 34, 65–6
photoelectric detectors 60–61
photometry 70–76
PIR (passive infra-red detector) 60–61
planning authority 14, 15
planning a lighting project 13–19
presence detector 60–61
professional advisors 3, 14, 15, 16
project planning 13–19
projectors 34–5
protection of building and contents 17, 83
pulpits 45, 60

purpose–made fittings 39

reading, lighting for 2, 8, 41–2
reflectance 50, 73–5
replacement lighting 13–19, 63–4
reredoses 45–6
rood screens 45–6

safety considerations 13–14, 19, 39, 51–3, 88
safety lighting 68–9
security lighting 5, 36, 54, 61, 68–9
selective lighting 41, 42, 43–8
sight problems and lighting 9, 42
site trials 50, 83
sodium lamps 27–8
solar dial time switches 61–2
sources of light 20–32
sparkle of chandeliers 36–7
specialist advice 3, 14, 15, 16
specification 16–17
spill light 42
spires 53
spotlights 34–5, 49
  aiming 64–5

stage lighting 9, 48
stained glass 1, 9, 47–8, 53
stall–mounted lights 44–5
striplights 25–6
switches 55–60
  time 61–2

techniques, lighting 48–50
tendering 17
Thompson levels 67–8
time switches 61–2
towers 53
track fixing 39
trees and external fittings 51, 53
tungsten–halogen lamps 23–4
  see also incandescent lamps

uplighters 39, 49
  buried 35–6

vision problems, and lighting 9, 42
voltage control dimmers 57–8

wall brackets 34
Wiring of Churches 17, 69, 82, 87